OPPOSING
VIEWPOINTS®
SERIES

D0911043

Social Security

Other Books of Related Interest:

"Congress shall make no law . . . abridging the freedom of speech, or of the press."

First Amendment to the U.S. Constitution

The basic foundation of our democracy is the First Amendment guarantee of freedom of expression. The Opposing Viewpoints Series is dedicated to the concept of this basic freedom and the idea that it is more important to practice it than to enshrine it.

OPPOSING
VIEWPOINTS®
SERIES

Social Security

Mitchell Young, Book Editor

GREENHAVEN PRESS
A part of Gale, Cengage Learning

GALE
CENGAGE Learning™

Detroit • New York • San Francisco • New Haven, Conn • Waterville, Maine • London

Christine Nasso, *Publisher*
Elizabeth Des Chenes, *Managing Editor*

© 2010 Greenhaven Press, a part of Gale, Cengage Learning

Gale and Greenhaven Press are registered trademarks used herein under license.

For more information, contact:
Greenhaven Press
27500 Drake Rd.
Farmington Hills, MI 48331-3535
Or you can visit our Internet site at gale.cengage.com

For product information and technology assistance, contact us at

Gale Customer Support, 1-800-877-4253
For permission to use material from this text or product, submit all requests online at www.cengage.com/permissions

Further permissions questions can be emailed to permissionrequest@cengage.com

Articles in Greenhaven Press anthologies are often edited for length to meet page requirements. In addition, original titles of these works are changed to clearly present the main thesis and to explicitly indicate the author's opinion. Every effort is made to ensure that Greenhaven Press accurately reflects the original intent of the authors. Every effort has been made to trace the owners of copyrighted material.

Cover image Tom Grill/Photographer's Choice RF/Getty Images.

LIBRARY OF CONGRESS CATALOGING-IN-PUBLICATION DATA

Social security / Mitchell Young, book editor.
 p. cm. -- (Opposing viewpoints)
 Includes bibliographical references and index.
 ISBN 978-0-7377-4856-7 (hardcover) -- ISBN 978-0-7377-4857-4 (pbk.)
 1. Social security--United States--Juvenile literature. I. Young, Mitchell.
 HD7125.S584 2010
 368.4'300973--dc22

2009052259

Printed in the United States of America
1 2 3 4 5 6 7 14 13 12 11 10

Contents

Chapter 2: How Should the Social Security System Be Reformed?

Chapter 3: How Does Social Security Affect Different Social Groups?

Chapter 4: How Do Other Countries Approach Social Security?

Why Consider Opposing Viewpoints?

> *"The only way in which a human being can make some approach to knowing the whole of a subject is by hearing what can be said about it by persons of every variety of opinion and studying all modes in which it can be looked at by every character of mind. No wise man ever acquired his wisdom in any mode but this."*
>
> *John Stuart Mill*

In our media-intensive culture it is not difficult to find differing opinions. Thousands of newspapers and magazines and dozens of radio and television talk shows resound with differing points of view. The difficulty lies in deciding which opinion to agree with and which "experts" seem the most credible. The more inundated we become with differing opinions and claims, the more essential it is to hone critical reading and thinking skills to evaluate these ideas. Opposing Viewpoints books address this problem directly by presenting stimulating debates that can be used to enhance and teach these skills. The varied opinions contained in each book examine many different aspects of a single issue. While examining these conveniently edited opposing views, readers can develop critical thinking skills such as the ability to compare and contrast authors' credibility, facts, argumentation styles, use of persuasive techniques, and other stylistic tools. In short, the Opposing Viewpoints Series is an ideal way to attain the higher-level thinking and reading skills so essential in a culture of diverse and contradictory opinions.

In addition to providing a tool for critical thinking, Opposing Viewpoints books challenge readers to question their own strongly held opinions and assumptions. Most people form their opinions on the basis of upbringing, peer pressure, and personal, cultural, or professional bias. By reading carefully balanced opposing views, readers must directly confront new ideas as well as the opinions of those with whom they disagree. This is not to simplistically argue that everyone who reads opposing views will—or should—change his or her opinion. Instead, the series enhances readers' understanding of their own views by encouraging confrontation with opposing ideas. Careful examination of others' views can lead to the readers' understanding of the logical inconsistencies in their own opinions, perspective on why they hold an opinion, and the consideration of the possibility that their opinion requires further evaluation.

Evaluating Other Opinions

To ensure that this type of examination occurs, Opposing Viewpoints books present all types of opinions. Prominent spokespeople on different sides of each issue as well as well-known professionals from many disciplines challenge the reader. An additional goal of the series is to provide a forum for other, less known, or even unpopular viewpoints. The opinion of an ordinary person who has had to make the decision to cut off life support from a terminally ill relative, for example, may be just as valuable and provide just as much insight as a medical ethicist's professional opinion. The editors have two additional purposes in including these less known views. One, the editors encourage readers to respect others' opinions—even when not enhanced by professional credibility. It is only by reading or listening to and objectively evaluating others' ideas that one can determine whether they are worthy of consideration. Two, the inclusion of such viewpoints encourages the important critical thinking skill of objectively evaluating an author's credentials and bias. This evaluation will illuminate an author's reasons for taking a particular stance on an issue and will aid in readers' evaluation of the author's ideas.

It is our hope that these books will give readers a deeper understanding of the issues debated and an appreciation of the complexity of even seemingly simple issues when good and honest people disagree. This awareness is particularly important in a democratic society such as ours in which people· enter into public debate to determine the common good. Those with whom one disagrees should not be regarded as enemies but rather as people whose views deserve careful examination and may shed light on one's own.

Thomas Jefferson once said that "difference of opinion leads to inquiry, and inquiry to truth." Jefferson, a broadly educated man, argued that "if a nation expects to be ignorant and free . . . it expects what never was and never will be." As individuals and as a nation, it is imperative that we consider the opinions of others and examine them with skill and discernment. The Opposing Viewpoints Series is intended to help readers achieve this goal.

David L. Bender and Bruno Leone,
Founders

Introduction

> *"We have tried to frame a law which will give some measure of protection to the average citizen and to his family against the loss of a job and against poverty-ridden old age."*
>
> President Franklin D. Roosevelt,
> upon signing the Social Security
> Act of 1935

Established during the Great Depression, the United States Social Security system is the key means of support for the elderly as well as for those who cannot work due to disability. Since its inception, the government-run pension program has dramatically decreased rates of poverty among elderly Americans. However, changes in the demographics of American society and increased eligibility for benefits have put Social Security under stress. Most pension policy experts agree that the system faces difficulties, but there is controversy over how severe those difficulties are and how best to overcome them.

Prior to 1900, there was little in the way of a formal, government-run pension program in the United States. Yet there was agitation for the creation of one as industrialization broke the ties of the extended family, which had been the chief provider for the elderly in a largely rural, nineteenth-century America. Germany, another nation changing from a rural to an urban society, instituted a national pension program in 1889, and the United States government granted a pension to all Union veterans of the Civil War in 1906. The latter pension applied to only 0.6 percent of the population, however. Throughout the first decades of the twentieth century, Americans relied on family, private savings, and company pensions for economic security in old age.

The Great Depression of the 1930s was the real catalyst for the creation of a national Social Security system that would cover nearly all Americans. Many newly unemployed workers lost what they had earned in the way of private pensions when their former employers failed. Self-employed farmers, who before the economic crisis would have relied on income from their property and the aid of family in old age, were forced off the land through bank foreclosures or the ecological disaster of the Dust Bowl. A variety of populist campaigns, such as the Townsend movement in California and the Bigelow plan in Ohio, sprang up around the country demanding a government-run old-age pension system.

This pressure led to the Social Security Act of 1935. Promoted by the Franklin D. Roosevelt administration, the act's centerpiece was Title II, "Federal Old-Age Benefits," which provided a federal pension to nearly all workers over age 65. The amount received by each individual depended on how much they contributed to the system over their working life. This differentiated it from a welfare program, where money is given out purely on the basis of need; workers thus "earned" their benefits. The system implemented was not an individual retirement savings program, however, but rather a so-called pay-as-you-go (PAYGO, for short) system where active workers' payroll taxes fund retirees' benefits.

Over the years the Social Security system has expanded in both dollar amount of benefits paid and in terms of categories of eligible beneficiaries. Even after the Social Security Act was signed, state and local government assistance to the elderly outweighed the federal program. In 1951, however, payments were increased, making the program the primary source of government assistance to retirees. In 1954 disability benefits were added for workers who had contributed to the system but who had been injured or otherwise incapacitated before age 65. In 1961, Medicare, a government medical insurance program for those over 65, was introduced. The last major expansion of the Social Security system came in 1972, when Supplemental Security Income (SSI), was introduced. It bestowed benefits on disabled persons who had never contributed to the system through payroll taxes.

Although the number of beneficiaries continued to grow, the trend of adding more categories of eligible beneficiaries ended in the 1980s. One of the chief reasons was demographic; Americans were no longer having large families and policymakers realized that there would be fewer workers in the future to support an ever-growing number of retirees. As a result there was some "retrenchment" of eligibility requirements; for the disabled in particular the focus changed from benefits to occupational training that would allow them to participate in the workforce. Social Security payroll taxes were raised in order to pay for the retirement of the "Baby Boom" generation—those Americans born between 1945 and 1964. For younger generations the age of eligibility for benefits was set to increase gradually from 65 to 67 years of age.

Despite these changes, the government's actuaries—the officials responsible for making financial predictions—remain concerned about Social Security's long-term solvency. With smaller families and increasing longevity, it was inevitable that future workers in a PAYGO system would be paying more taxes to support an ever-growing pool of retirees. A proposed alternative to this system has been privatization—replacing the PAYGO system with individual mandatory retirement savings accounts. Proponents of such accounts claim that the accounts will return more money to retirees and boost the economy's overall performance while eliminating the problem of too few workers funding too many pensioners. Privatization opponents claim that such programs are expensive to manage and have failed to alleviate the pension crises in the countries that have adopted them.

Opposing Viewpoints: Social Security explores different views on how to handle the challenges faced by the nation's retirement system in four chapters titled: Does a Social Security Crisis Exist? How Should the Social Security System Be Reformed? How Does Social Security Affect Different Social Groups? and How Do Other Countries Approach Social Security? Each of the chapters shows the lively debate over how best to improve America's primary retirement and disability insurance program.

CHAPTER 1

Does a Social Security Crisis Exist?

Chapter Preface

The populations of advanced industrialized economies around the world are aging. Women are having fewer children, and people are living longer. This means that in the very near future countries such as the United States, Japan, and Germany will have fewer and fewer active workers supporting more and more retirees. For most government retirement systems this means trouble, because they are supported by a tax on current employees. A shrinking pool of workers and a growing number of senior citizens receiving benefits means that changes have to be made in order to maintain the financial solvency of these so-called pay-as-you-go (PAYGO) retirement systems.

Most who study retirement policy agree that PAYGO systems are headed for difficulties. American experts and commentators disagree, however, on how severe the problem is for the United States and its main government-run retirement program—Social Security. There is a pool of money, the Social Security Trust Fund, which has been built up over decades as workers paid more into the system than was paid out to beneficiaries. This reserve is designed to help the United States through approaching demographic difficulties, particularly the retirement of the large, post–World War II "baby-boom" generation. Skeptics such as retired investment banker Peter G. Peterson argue that the trust fund is a myth, that the funds it contains are meaningless IOUs issued by one government agency (the Treasury) to another (the Social Security Administration). According to Peterson, this will become evident in the mid-2010s as Social Security's payouts start to exceed its income. Peterson predicts:

> "Because this is a Pay-As-You-Go system, Congress would then have to raise taxes, cut other spending or borrow from the public to redeem the IOU's . . . or else take a heavy

hatchet to Social Security and Medicare at the very moment the huge boomer generation is moving into its elder years."

Others, such as liberal commentator Matthew Yglesias, argue that fears about Social Security's financial situation are exaggerated for political and ideological purposes. Yglesias notes:

"Social Security is healthy and successful. There is no crisis. The president and the Republicans in Congress are trying to scare the American people in order to destroy the most successful program in American history."

According to Yglesias, what Peterson claims are mere IOUs are "U.S. Treasury bonds, considered far and wide to be the safest investment in the world." With these assets available, the Social Security system looks solvent for decades to come, he asserts.

Whether Social Security is indeed facing a crisis is an important issue, as it affects decisions about whether the system needs reforming. Those who see a crisis generally want radical reform to be implemented soon. Those who think Social Security's problems are more transitory difficulties rather than a crisis think that minor adjustments can maintain the system's solvency. The following chapter contains a variety of views on how demographic changes are affecting PAYGO systems, whether the changes are indeed causing a crisis, and how developments that affect Social Security shape and are shaped by the world of politics.

> *"The combined [Social Security trust] funds are . . . projected to become exhausted and thus unable to pay scheduled benefits in full on a timely basis in 2037."*

Social Security Will Be Bankrupt by 2037 Unless Reformed

Board of Trustees of the Federal Old-Age and Survivors Insurance and Federal Disability Insurance Trust Funds

The Social Security system has a board of trustees to oversee its operations. The following viewpoint is excerpted from the board's annual report for 2009. Its researchers estimated how many workers will be paying into the system and how many people will be receiving benefits for a "75-year window" into the future. Using intermediate assumptions about the number of retirees, the growth of the working population, and the growth of economic output—measured as gross domestic product, or GDP— the board finds that the system will be out of funds in 2037, well before the projected window is closed.

Jason J. Fichtner et al. *Annual Report of the Board of Trustees of the Federal Old-Age and Survivors Insurance and Federal Disability Insurance Trust Funds*. Washington, DC: Government Printing Office, 2009.

As you read, consider the following questions:

1. According to the authors, what are the two main components of the U.S. Social Security System?

2. When, according to the authors, will the Social Security system begin to pay out more in benefits than it receives in tax income?

3. What accounts for about half of the reduction of the 2009 estimated actuarial balance of the Social Security system compared with what was estimated in 2008, as reported by the authors?

The Old-Age, Survivors, and Disability Insurance (OASDI) program in the United States makes available a basic level of monthly income upon the attainment of retirement eligibility age, death, or disability by insured workers. The OASDI program consists of two separate parts that pay benefits to workers and their families—Old-Age and Survivors Insurance (OASI) and Disability Insurance (DI). Under OASI, monthly benefits are paid to retired workers and their families and to survivors of deceased workers. Under DI, monthly benefits are paid to disabled workers and their families. . . .

At the end of 2008, almost 51 million people were receiving benefits: 35 million retired workers and dependents of retired workers, 6 million survivors of deceased workers, and 9 million disabled workers and dependents of disabled workers. During the year, an estimated 162 million people had earnings covered by Social Security and paid payroll taxes. Total benefits paid in 2008 were $615 billion. Total income was $805 billion, and assets held in special issue U.S. Treasury securities grew to $2.4 trillion.

Outlook for the Future

The OASI Trust Fund and the combined OASI and DI Trust Funds are adequately financed over the next 10 years under the intermediate assumptions. The DI Trust Fund is expected to remain solvent over the next 10 years, but does not satisfy the short-range test of financial adequacy because assets are estimated to fall below 100 percent of annual expenditures by the beginning of 2014. The combined assets of the OASI and DI Trust Funds are projected to increase from $2,419 billion at the beginning of 2009, or 354 percent of annual expenditures, to $3,874 billion at the beginning of 2018, or 338 percent of annual expenditures in that year. Combined assets were projected for last year's [2008] report to rise to 369 percent of annual expenditures at the beginning of 2009, and 378 percent at the beginning of 2018.

Under the intermediate assumptions, OASDI cost will increase more rapidly than tax income between about 2012 and 2030 because the retirement of the baby-boom generation will cause the number of beneficiaries to rise much faster than the labor force. After 2030, increases in life expectancy and the continued relatively low fertility rates experienced since the baby boom will generally cause Social Security system costs to increase relative to tax income, but more slowly. Annual cost will exceed tax income starting in 2016, at which time the annual gap will be covered with cash from redemptions of special obligations of the Treasury that make up the trust fund assets until these assets are exhausted in 2037. Individually, the DI fund is projected to be exhausted in 2020 and the OASI fund in 2039. For the 75-year projection period, the actuarial [statistically calculated] deficit is 2.00 percent of taxable payroll, 0.30 percentage point larger than in last year's report. The open group unfunded obligation for OASDI over the 75-year period is $5.3 trillion in present value, and is $0.9 trillion more than the measured level of a year ago. In the absence of any changes in assumptions, methods, and starting values, the unfunded obligation would have risen to about $4.6 trillion due to the change in the valuation date.

The OASDI annual cost rate is projected to increase from 12.35 percent of taxable payroll in 2009, to 16.76 percent in 2030, and to 17.68 percent in 2083, a level that is 4.34 percent of taxable payroll more than the projected income rate for 2083. For last year's report, the OASDI cost for 2083 was estimated at 17.54 percent, or 4.25 percent of payroll more than the annual income rate for that year. Expressed in relation to the projected gross domestic product (GDP), OASDI cost is estimated to rise from the current level of 4.8 percent of GDP to 6.1 percent in 2030, and then to peak at almost 6.2 percent in 2034. Thereafter, OASDI cost as a percent of GDP is projected to decline, reaching a level around 5.8 percent for the period 2050 through 2083.

Tax Increases Necessary

The worsening of the long-range actuarial status of the OASDI program indicated in this report is principally the result of projected lower levels of economic activity that reflect the recent economic downturn and updated data, and faster reductions in mortality assumed in the longer term. Changes in the economic assumptions and the mortality assumptions contribute to about the same degree to the reduction in the program's actuarial balance.

Under the long-range intermediate assumptions, annual cost will begin to exceed tax income in 2016 for the combined OASDI Trust Funds. The combined funds are then projected to become exhausted and thus unable to pay scheduled benefits in full on a timely basis in 2037. The separate DI Trust Fund, however, is projected to become exhausted in 2020.

For the combined OASDI Trust Funds to remain solvent throughout the 75-year projection period, the combined payroll tax rate could be increased during the period in a manner equivalent to an immediate and permanent increase of 2.01 percentage points, benefits could be reduced during the period in a manner equivalent to an immediate and permanent

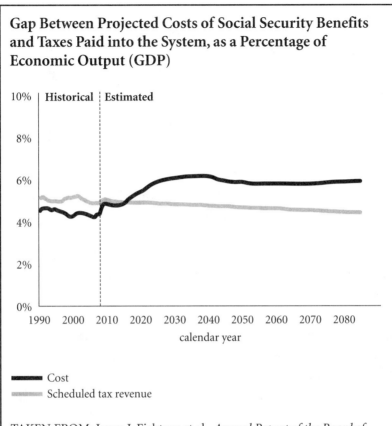

Gap Between Projected Costs of Social Security Benefits and Taxes Paid into the System, as a Percentage of Economic Output (GDP)

TAKEN FROM: Jason J. Fichtner et al., *Annual Report of the Board of Trustees of the Federal Old-Age and Survivors Insurance and Federal Disability Insurance Trust Funds*, 2009.

reduction of 13.3 percent, general revenue transfers equivalent to $5.3 trillion in present value could be made during the period, or some combination of approaches could be adopted. Significantly larger changes would be required to maintain solvency beyond 75 years.

For this year's [2009] intermediate projections, real GDP starts at a lower level than was assumed last year for 2008, declines through the second quarter of 2009, levels off in the third quarter, and then begins to grow, reaching the projected stable, sustainable path by the end of 2015. These revised economic assumptions account for about half of the estimated reduction in the program's actuarial balance relative to last year's report. The effect of the recession on the actuarial balance would be smaller than projected in this report if the recovery were such that economic output substantially overshoots the projected sustainable path, a phenomenon observed in some past business cycles.

Timely Action Needed

The projected trust fund deficits should be addressed in a timely way so that necessary changes can be phased in gradually and workers can be given time to plan for them. Implementing changes sooner will allow their effects to be spread over more generations. Social Security plays a critical role in the lives of 52 million beneficiaries and 160 million covered workers and their families in 2009. With informed discussion, creative thinking, and timely legislative action, present and future Congresses and Presidents can ensure that Social Security continues to protect future generations.

> "Whether intentionally or unintentionally, those who assert that the 'surplus in Social Security is disappearing' are misleading the American public."

Social Security Remains Financially Strong

National Committee to Preserve Social Security and Medicare

The mission of the National Committee to Preserve Social Security and Medicare is to protect the financial well-being of retired Americans. It believes that maintaining the Social Security system is the primary means of achieving that mission.

In the following viewpoint, the committee argues that the government's annual report for 2009 shows that Social Security remains strong. It claims that the recession has not drastically affected the system because the government focuses on the long term and has already accounted for ups and downs in the national economy. The economic downturn's effect on Americans' private savings shows that a government-run Social Security system is vital for retirees' financial security.

National Committee to Preserve Social Security and Medicare, Government Relations and Policy, *Analysis of 2009 Annual Report of the Social Security Trustees.* Washington, DC: Author, 2009. Reproduced by permission.

As you read, consider the following questions:

1. What does the Social Security Administration do when payroll tax revenues exceed benefits paid out, according to the author?

2. How, according to the committee, has the recession affected the long-term financial health of Social Security?

3. What are the two types of surpluses mentioned by the author in discussions of Social Security?

The Social Security Act created a Board of Trustees to oversee the Old-Age, Survivors and Disability Insurance Trust Funds (OASDI), popularly known as the Social Security Trust Funds. Each year the Trustees issue a report on the financial status of the Trust Funds. The report is a snapshot of the health of the funds in the short range (10 years) and in the long range (75 years). With the help of the Social Security Administration actuaries [insurance experts], the Trustees estimate the income and expenditures of the Fund, taking into account projections of both demographic and economic factors.

The Social Security Trust Funds are considered to be in long-range balance when the income to the Funds exceeds expenditures over 75 years. When income does not meet expenditures in the long run, there is a shortfall, or deficit. Income, expenditures and balances are expressed in both dollars and as a "percent of payroll," meaning the percent of all wages or self-employment income subject to taxation.

How Social Security Is Financed

Social Security is financed mainly through payroll taxes on wages and self-employment income. Employees and employers each make contributions equal to 6.2 percent of wages, up to a wage cap of $106,800 in 2009 that ordinarily increases with the growth in the nationwide average wage. The wage cap was originally set at an amount that would tax about 90 percent of all wage income in the United States. However, wages at the high end of the income scale have risen faster than average paychecks in recent years, so today the cap only covers about 83 percent of wages.

The self-employed contribute the equivalent of the combined employer and employee tax rates, which is 12.4 percent. They are then allowed to deduct the equivalent of the employer's share from their income taxes. Social Security also receives a small amount of revenue from income taxes on Social Security benefits paid by retirees with higher incomes.

When working Americans pay their Social Security payroll taxes to the U.S. Treasury, those taxes are credited to the Social Security Trust Funds. Some of those taxes are paid out monthly in Social Security benefits. If income to the Trust Funds exceeds the value of benefits paid, then the Social Security Trust Funds are credited with the excess income. The income is used to purchase special issue U.S. government bonds that are backed by the full faith and credit of the United States. The bonds earn a rate of return similar to that earned by other long-term U.S. securities. An excess of annual income over expenditures results in an annual surplus. The accumulated annual surpluses become the total assets of the Trust Funds. Those assets earn interest and further increase the funds. These accumulated assets are commonly referred to as the Social Security "surplus" or "reserves."

According to the 2009 Trustees' report, income from Social Security payroll taxes will account for about 83 percent of Trust Fund income in 2008; income taxes paid on Social Security benefits will represent 2 percent, and interest on reserves will make up the remaining 14 percent.

At the end of 2008, nearly 51 million people were receiving benefits: 35 million retired workers and their dependents, 6 million survivors of deceased workers, and 9 million disabled workers and their dependents. During the last year an estimated 162 million workers had earnings covered by Social Security and paid payroll taxes. . . .

Financial Outlook Remains Strong

The Trustees project that the combined Old-Age, Survivor, and Disability (OASDI) Trust Fund will be able to pay full benefits until the year 2037. Thereafter, Social Security will have sufficient annual revenue to pay about 75 percent of benefits. Last year's [2008] Trustees' report predicted that Social Security would be able to pay full benefits until 2041 and 78 percent of benefits thereafter.

Social Security's accumulated assets continue to grow. For 2009, Social Security's reserves are projected to rise to $2.6 trillion.

The recession has had only a modest impact on the long-range solvency of Social Security. That is because the length of the downturn is relatively short when compared to the long-range 75-year projection period for Social Security. In general, the Social Security Trustees already take into account the impact of economic cycles when making their long-term projections. However, this year [2009] the Trustees have projected slightly lower growth in the Gross Domestic Product (GDP) after the economy recovers. The chief reasons for the change from 2041 to 2037 are the lower GDP growth and an assumed faster reduction in the mortality rate.

Year-to-year fluctuation in the long-range date for insolvency is expected and this year's projection is well within the range of estimates for the last decade. In the 1990s, the date on which the Trust Fund was expected to be unable to pay full benefits hovered around 2030. In this decade, the projected date has been between 2037 and 2042. In fact, the Trustees projected in the year 2000 that the Trust Fund would be unable to pay full benefits in 2037. This demonstrates that assumptions about demographics and the economy can alter

Key Dates for the Old-Age, Survivors, and Disability Insurance Trust Funds

	Old-Age and Survivors Insurance	Disability Insurance	Old-Age, Survivors, and Disability Insurance
First year outgo exceeds income excluding interest	2017	2005	2016
First year outgo exceeds income including interest	2025	2009	2024
Year trust fund assets are exhausted	2039	2020	2037

TAKEN FROM: "Analysis of 2009 Annual Report of the Social Security Trustees." Washington, D.C.: National Committee to Preserve Social Security and Medicare, Government Relations and Policy, 2009.

projections significantly, but that the current estimate does not differ significantly from estimates over the last decade.

The report of the Trustees confirms that the recession has not placed a significant strain on the Social Security Trust Fund, as some assert. Some conservative analysts and policymakers have tried to make it appear as though the recession has slashed the surplus. One observer argued that Social Security's surplus would nearly disappear by next year.

Social Security's surplus is not disappearing. Due in part to the economic downturn, the 2009 report projects smaller short-term annual surpluses in the Old-Age, Survivors and Disability (OASDI) Trust Fund when compared to the short-term annual surplus projected in last year's report. This means that the Social Security Trust Fund will not be loaning as much money to the general government as had been projected prior to the recession, but it does not reduce the Trust Fund's ability to finance benefits.

Less Government Borrowing

Under the 2009 Trustees' projections, the general government will be able to borrow from Social Security $76 billion less this year and $87 billion less in 2010 than was projected in last year's report. The 2009 Trustees' report projects that the short-term OASDI "annual surpluses" will be lower than projected in last year's report. In this year's report, the Trustees projected an annual surplus of $137 billion for the year 2009 and $138 billion for 2010. Last year, prior to the economic downturn, the Trustees had projected a somewhat larger annual surplus of $213 billion for 2009 and $225 billion for 2010.

The above figures include *all* income and outgo of the OASDI Trust Fund. Some fiscal analysts fail to count as income the interest on the securities held by the Trust Fund, arguing that it is an intergovernmental transfer. While the source of that income may be general government funds, that interest is *owed by statute* to the Trust Fund.

While the Trustees' report shows that annual cash flow, excluding interest, to the Social Security Trust Fund will go negative in 2016 instead of 2017, the Trust Fund will continue to pay full benefits from continuing payroll taxes and other receipts to the Trust Fund, including interest owed on the assets held by the Trust Fund.

According to the new projections, Social Security will be able to continue paying benefits with income, including interest, until 2024. After 2024, the federal government will have to start repaying the loans that the Social Security Trust Fund has made to the general fund. Revenue to Social Security from the payroll tax and other receipts, including the repayment to the Trust Fund of the loans made to the general government, will finance full benefits through 2037.

We Need Social Security

Whether intentionally or unintentionally, those who assert that the "surplus in Social Security is disappearing" are misleading the American public. In fact, Social Security has two types of surpluses: the "annual surplus" and the "total assets" (sometimes also known as the "surplus"). An "annual surplus" occurs in any year in which the revenue to Social Security that year exceeds the outgo for the year. As those annual surpluses accumulate over time, they become the "total assets" of the Social Security Trust Fund. Because many people refer to those accumulated assets as Social Security's surplus, they may incorrectly conclude that the reduction in projected annual surpluses over the next few years means that Social Security's total-assets surplus, which is $2.6 trillion in 2009, is disappearing in the short term and that Social Security will soon be unable to pay benefits. The truth is that, even after taking into account the impact of the recession, the assets held by the Trust Fund will continue to permit payment of full benefits until 2037.

Current economic conditions have had a devastating effect on the retirement savings of millions of Americans, leaving them with significant reductions in their 401(k)s and other retirement vehicles. At the same time housing values have dropped dramatically. Social Security was created in times much like today to provide Americans with a foundation of security they could count on in uncertain economic times. Social Security smoothes the risks of these economic cycles over large groups of people and long periods of time, and it remains the most secure retirement income in America.

> "The aging of America has created a situation in which relatively fewer workers will be asked to support a growing retired population."

Smaller Families and Increasing Longevity Threaten Social Security

Gayle L. Reznik, Dave Shoffner, and David A. Weaver

In the following viewpoint, three researchers from the Social Security Administration discuss what declines in fertility and increasing life span mean for the nation's retirement system. Social Security is a "pay as you go" (PAYGO) system, not a retirement savings account; current workers must support, through their payroll taxes, retirees and others receiving benefits. Because women are having fewer children, projections show that in 2040 there will be just over two workers for each beneficiary, down from almost three and a half workers per beneficiary in 2000. The authors discuss the pros and cons of increasing retirement age as one way to mitigate this situation.

Gayle L. Reznik, Dave Shoffner, and David A. Weaver, "Coping with the Demographic Challenge: Fewer Children and Living Longer," *Social Security Bulletin*, vol. 66, no. 4, 2005, pp. 37–45.

As you read, consider the following questions:

1. How do fertility rates change, in comparison with changes in life expectancy, according to the authors?

2. According to projections cited by Reznik, Shoffner, and Weaver, what will be the life expectancy for someone turning sixty-five in 2040?

3. How do the average education and lifetime earnings of early retirees compare with those who work until age sixty-five, in the authors' opinion?

Americans are living longer and are having fewer children. Together these factors result in the aging of the U.S. population and a subsequent strain on the Social Security system. This demographic challenge has been recognized by policy analysts as well as policymakers. President [George W.] Bush, in his 2005 State of the Union Address, highlighted this problem, saying:

> In today's world, people are living longer and, therefore, drawing benefits longer. And those benefits are scheduled to rise dramatically over the next few decades. And instead of sixteen workers paying in for every beneficiary, right now it's only about three workers. And over the next few decades that number will fall to just two workers per beneficiary. With each passing year, fewer workers are paying ever-higher benefits to an ever-larger number of retirees. . . .

An Aging Population

In 1950, 8 percent of the total population was aged 65 or older. That share was 12 percent in 2005 and is projected to reach 23 percent by 2080. The elderly population will have more than doubled as a percentage of the total population in just over 100 years. At the same time, the working-age population will have shrunk, from 60 percent in 2005 to 54 percent in 2080.

These demographic changes can be traced to declining fertility rates as well as increasing life expectancies. At the start of the baby boom (1946), the average number of children born to a woman in her lifetime was 2.86. By the end of the baby boom (1964), that number had increased to 3.17. The fertility rate was much lower in the postboomer years, although the rate has increased since 1980 and is projected to decline slightly in the coming decades.

Unlike the fertility trends, which exhibit large swings over particular periods, life expectancy exhibits a steady increase. In 1960, a 65-year-old individual could expect to live another 15.5 years. By 2000, life expectancy at age 65 had risen by 2.5 years. Projections indicate further gains of similar magnitude by 2040, at which point 65-year-olds can expect to live an additional 20.4 years.

Immigration also plays a role in the age structure of the population. Compared with earlier decades, net immigration has increased in recent years. Because immigrants tend to be younger and have higher fertility rates than the general population, immigration mitigates the aging of the population. Without immigration the aging trend would be more pronounced.

Challenges Facing Social Security

Rising life expectancy is a positive development in that it gives people more years to enjoy life, but adjustments and adaptations are needed so that people will have the means to enjoy their extra years. Rising life expectancy, along with falling fertility rates, is also a primary cause of the financial difficulties that social insurance systems face in the United States and throughout the world. [According to the program's Board of Trustees] "Under current law the cost of Social Security will soon begin to increase faster than the program's income, because of the aging of the baby-boom generation, expected continuing low fertility, and increasing life expectancy."

The aging of America has created a situation in which relatively fewer workers will be asked to support a growing retired population. The historical and projected ratios of workers to beneficiaries, measured as the number of workers in Social Security–covered employment divided by the number of Social Security beneficiaries . . . is fairly stable in years the boomers are in the workforce (1980–2005) but is substantially lower when the boomers are in their retirement years (2020–2040).

The worker-to-beneficiary ratio has fallen from 5.1 in 1960 to 3.3 in 2005. Some of the historical decline is related to the natural maturing of a pay-as-you-go social insurance program, but the projected future decline is due to the aging of the U.S. population. This ratio is of fundamental importance to the long-run fiscal health of the U.S. Social Security program. With currently scheduled tax rates and benefits, the system needs a worker-to-beneficiary ratio of about 2.8 to function at a pay-as-you-go level (meaning that tax revenue approximately equals benefit payments). The Social Security Trustees project that the ratio will slip below this level by 2020 and will fall to only 2.1 workers per beneficiary by 2040. The current Social Security program is not a strict pay-as-you-go program because a sizable trust fund exists. Projections indicate, however, that the trust fund will be exhausted in 2040, and the low worker-to-beneficiary ratio will present a significant challenge to policymakers.

Policy Options for Solvency

In the United States, a number of analysts believe that retirement benefits should be adjusted to reflect the fact that people are living longer—a concept referred to as *longevity indexing*. Edward M. Gramlich, chairman of the 1994–1996 Advisory Council on Social Security and a former Federal Reserve Governor, argues that a "'slight cut in the growth of future benefits' is a fair way to deal with the fact that retirees are

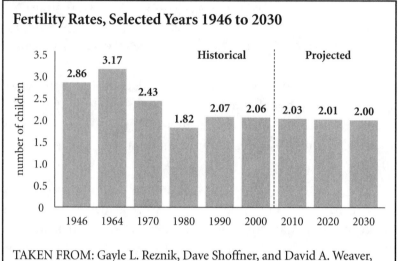

Fertility Rates, Selected Years 1946 to 2030

TAKEN FROM: Gayle L. Reznik, Dave Shoffner, and David A. Weaver, "Coping with the Demographic Challenge: Fewer Children and Living Longer," *Social Security Bulletin*, vol. 66, no. 4, 2005.

likely to live longer—and collect more in benefits—than in 1935, when the retirement age was set at 65." Proponents of longevity indexing point to the fact that, because people are living longer, yearly benefits can be reduced in a proportion equivalent to rising life expectancy and average lifetime benefits will remain constant. . . .

However, there are also important critiques to proposals to reduce benefits in proportion to rising life expectancy. Most important is the great variety in the types of jobs people have and their reasons for retiring when they do. Quantitative research corroborates the concern that many early retirees face greater health and mortality risks. Hilary Waldron of the Social Security Administration's Office of Policy used data from federal surveys matched with administrative records to compare men who retired early with men who retired at the normal retirement age of 65. She found that "the majority of early retirees are in poorer health and have higher mortality risk than that of age 65 retirees, and only a minority have health and mortality risk as good as that of age 65 retirees. . . .

Some, but not all, of this difference is explained by early retirees being more likely to have low education and average lifetime earnings." Further, [other researchers] suggest that many individuals develop health problems, suffer job losses, or take on caregiving responsibilities in the years around the age of early eligibility. Thus, the evidence shows that a reduction in benefits in proportion to rising life expectancy has the potential to disadvantage some retirees, including some who are vulnerable to economic hardship.

> "People living longer is a flimsy justifi-
> cation for weakening pensions and
> compelling older people to work more."

False Beliefs Have Led to a Social Security Scare

Teresa Ghilarducci

Teresa Ghilarducci is the Schwartz Professor of Economic Policy Analysis at the New School for Social Research in New York City. In the following viewpoint she attacks what she calls "three common beliefs" that Americans have about the Social Security system. She maintains that people living longer is a result of retirement benefits, not the cause of a crisis. She argues that there will be no labor shortages and that pension coverage could be extended to more people by eliminating the tax subsidies for individual retirement accounts—such as 401(k) plans—which mainly benefit high-income people.

As you read, consider the following questions:

1. What does the author imply caused the increases in longevity seen in the United States?

Teresa Ghilarducci, *When I'm Sixty-Four: The Plot Against Pensions and the Plan to Save Them*. Princeton, NJ: Princeton University Press, 2008. Copyright © 2008 by Princeton University Press. Reproduced by permission.

2. What are the three ways pension income could become more insecure, as suggested by Ghilarducci?

3. According to the author, does the percentage of individuals receiving pensions improve as individual retirement plans overtake defined benefit pensions such as Social Security?

A mericans seem to believe these three ideas:

1. Life expectancy is increasing, so we should work longer.

2. The United States will suffer labor shortages as the population ages.

3. Pensions are unaffordable.

These three propositions are invalid, and for these reasons: People retiring earlier could be the reason for increased life expectancy; a lower future rate of growth in the labor force will increase wages, not cause labor shortages; and there are other ways (besides shifting tax breaks away from high-income employees, who would save without the subsidy, to middle- and lower-income workers who would benefit from them) in which governments and employers play a strong role in a functioning pension system.

Let us consider each proposition.

First False Proposition

Americans should work longer because the are living longer. Using almost every measure—entry into the labor force at young ages, longer hours of work, relatively later retirement ages, and higher labor force participation of parents with young children—Americans work more than workers in most developed nations. Societies in different nations deal in different ways with the scarcity of time—time for work and time for leisure. Mothers with small children in the United States work more than mothers in France, the United Kingdom, Germany, and Japan. French and German workers have on average fewer years of education than U.S. workers, suggesting that French and German citizens start work sooner, but they also end their work careers at much younger ages. If Americans work longer and reduce their time in retirement, they will be pulling even further away from other nations in valuing leisure.

However, in the United States, as in any nation, not all groups are able to retire. Not everyone has enough pension savings. Not everyone lives to the same age. Here is the problem: life expectancy is increasing, yes—but not for everyone. There is a growing gap in longevity between those with college educations and those without.

Although large amounts of retirement leisure, through better pensions and longer lives, is a sign of a rich economy, the recent increases in the United States in the expected time in retirement resulted from longer lives, not from more valuable pensions. The largest leap in longevity rates came after 1965: when Medicare extended health insurance coverage to almost all the elderly; larger Social Security benefits reduced the adverse health effects of low income; and traditional pension plans let workers who wanted to, especially those in physically demanding jobs, retire before age sixty-five. People living longer is a flimsy justification for weakening pensions and compelling older people to work more. It is an anemic course of reasoning because the argument is based on the assumptions that (a) workers do not value free time as they age, and (b) older people can do the new jobs, and (c) people are not living longer because they are improving their health by retiring sooner.

Elderly Limited in Work Capacity

Assumption (a) is false because, as the nation grew richer, work hours fell and vacation time soared. Assumption (b) is false because there is little evidence that the ability of older

Americans' Work Effort Tops That of Most Nations

	Average Hours Worked per Year (1997–1998)	Average Education (in Years)	Labor Force Participation of Mothers
United States	1,966	12.7	68%
Japan	1,889	13.5	54%
Britain	1,731	13.2	62%
Germany	1,560	12.2	41%
France	1,634	10.7	68%

TAKEN FROM: Teresa Ghilarducci, *When I'm Sixty-Four: The Plot against Pensions and the Plan to Save Them*, Princeton, N.J.: Princeton University Press, 2008.

people to work longer has improved. Since 1981, the share of older workers reporting limitations in the ability to work stayed steady at between 15% and 18%. Jobs demanding heavy lifting, stooping and kneeling, and overall physical effort are declining, especially for men. However, older workers report a 17% increase in jobs involving a lot of stress and intense concentration. Older women report a 17% increase in jobs requiring good eyesight. As to whether the computer has made jobs easier for older workers, the jury is out.

As for why assumption (c) is false, consider this: Retirement time itself boosts longevity. Retired men do not age as fast—their health deteriorates at a slower pace than for men who are still working, but both are alike in many other ways. Retired women are in better health than they would have been had they still been working. This evidence suggests that longevity itself improved because people retired! If older people are compelled to stay in the labor force longer, this could reverse the progress society has made in increasing life expectancy for American people over age sixty-five. This is unfortunate for the less obvious reason that the impressive longevity improvements have shrunk what would otherwise have been a severe decrease in average retirement time. In short, as older people work more and experience more unemployment, they will likely encounter health difficulties, especially if they experience downward mobility in their status at work. They will become less able to do a job well, and they will have less time to care for themselves—sleeping, exercising, preparing and eating meals. So, instead of improved longevity being a reason why older people should work more, it is a fact that older people who worked less improved their longevity.

Second False Proposition

The United States will soon suffer labor shortages as the population ages. This proposition implies that there is a labor shortage and older people have to help solve it. This is false for several reasons.

One reason is that labor shortages simply do not exist. What is called a "shortage" in any market merely describes any situation where demand exceeds supply. Reasonably, employers reckon labor supply will meet labor demand only when wages increase or the job offer is made more attractive. To paraphrase Wharton Business School economist Peter Cappelli, this is unlikely to be a problem for public policy. Should pensions be made more insecure because the generation coming after the boomers (in 2008, the oldest baby boomer turns sixty-two and the youngest boomer turns forty-five) is smaller and employers would rather not raise wages? There are three ways pension income will become more insecure, thus making older workers more likely to work:

- the erosion of employment-linked defined benefit pension plans and development of a system of commercial, individual-based pensions (401(k) type plans) to replace them;

- the projected decline in Social Security benefits; and

- upward pressure on noninsured health care costs.

Third False Proposition

Pensions are unaffordable. Many argue that the greatest threat to pensions is the enormity of their expense, implying that pensions must shrink because they are not affordable. For example, Boston University's Laurence Kotlikoff and coauthor Scott Burns argue just that in their brisk-selling book, *The Coming Generational Storm*, a title that announces the boomers' retirement as if it will be a disaster as severe as a tsunami. The truth is that the money now spent on pensions is largely wasted and could be used to extend pension coverage to millions more Americans.

Yes, the government does spend a great deal on pensions— above the expense for Social Security programs and Medicare. The expense is through the system of tax breaks for voluntary employer and individual retirement plans: defined benefit plans, all defined contribution plans (including 401(k) plans), individual retirement accounts (IRAs), and other retirement savings vehicles. Contributions to these plans and investment earnings on the contributions are not taxed; only the pensions paid out at retirement are taxed, but commonly at a much lower tax rate than when the employee was working. The tax-favored treatment for retirement plans has been, until 2006, the largest of all categories of federal government tax expenditures. In 2009, taxes not collected on pension funds and contributions will be the federal government's second-to-largest tax expenditure. The government's largest tax expenditure will be employer contributions for medical health insurance premiums. Employers' contributions are government tax expenditures because the contributions are exempted from income tax. This means the government forgoes revenue and "spends" that forgone revenue on the tax break.

The Puzzle of Pensions

What remains puzzling is why, despite the huge and growing tax subsidy for pensions, pension coverage has stagnated. The puzzle is explained by the changing structure of the tax subsidy. The tax subsidy for 401(k) plans mostly benefits higher-income workers. Higher-income workers (and indirectly their employers) pay higher income tax rates under the progressive income tax structure; so a tax break is worth more to higher-income workers relative to the same tax break for lower-income workers. This means that workers at different earnings levels, say each contributing 10% of their salary to a pension plan, receive widely different tax breaks from the federal government.

If a worker does not participate in a pension plan, of course, he gets nothing from the federal program subsidizing pensions. . . . Among workers with pensions, it is the lower- and middle-income workers who are less likely to participate in 401(k) plans than in defined benefit plans. Thus, as 401(k) plans overtake defined benefit pensions, tax subsidies grow because pension coverage shifts to high earners, while overall pension coverage does not improve. This is a waste of taxpayers' money because tax policy toward employee benefits aims to meet public goals for retirement security. The tax breaks do not help households save more, increasing the nation's savings in proportion to national income. The $115 billion of tax expenditures for all retirement accounts in 2004 was equal to one-fourth of Social Security contributions. Rather than increasing savings, research suggests that tax breaks mostly induce high-income households to shift savings they already have in financial assets that are taxed to tax-favored accounts. . . .

A Cocktail of Solutions

Although these three propositions—people living longer should work longer, labor shortages will hurt the economy, and pensions are unaffordable for employers and government—are false, they nevertheless result in a cocktail of solutions that reduces pension security: raising the retirement age for Social Security, which reduces benefits; allowing defined benefit plans to collapse; and promoting defined contribution, 401(k)-type retirement accounts. These solutions fall short of what should be an efficient and low-cost retirement system that delivers adequate levels of pensions for workers at all income levels and for different life expectancies.

> *"Uncle Sam owes ... trillions to Social Security retirees and has to pay it back or look like just another deadbeat. That risk is the only 'crisis' facing Social Security."*

Politics Are Behind the Social Security Scare

William Greider

William Greider was a longtime reporter for the Washington Post. *His latest book,* Come Home America, *deals with the financial issues facing the country. In the following viewpoint, Greider argues that the stories of a crisis in Social Security are manufactured and points to Wall Street financier Pete Peterson as the chief culprit in creating the surrounding "hysteria." Greider maintains that the system is sound but that the government and big financial interests are worried that money borrowed from the trust fund, paid for by higher payroll taxes on workers, will soon have to be repaid.*

As you read, consider the following questions:

1. What is the total rate of Social Security tax on labor wages, according to Greider?

William Greider, "The Man Who Wants to Loot Social Security," *Nation*, March 2, 2009, pp. 12–14. Copyright © 2009 by The Nation Magazine/The Nation Company, Inc. Reproduced by permission.

2. What does the author say is the only way to hold down the costs of Medicaid and Medicare?

3. What does Greider propose as a model for a universal pension system?

Governing elites in Washington and Wall Street have devised a fiendishly clever "grand bargain" they want President [Barack] Obama to embrace in the name of "fiscal responsibility." The government, they argue, having spent billions on bailing out the banks, can recover its costs by looting the Social Security system. They are also targeting Medicare and Medicaid. The pitch sounds preposterous to millions of ordinary working people anxious about their economic security and worried about their retirement years. But an impressive armada is lined up to push the idea—Washington's leading think tanks, the prestige media, tax-exempt foundations, skillful propagandists posing as economic experts and a self-righteous billionaire spending his fortune to save the nation from the elderly.

Political Bait and Switch

These players are promoting a tricky way to whack Social Security benefits, but to do it behind closed doors so the public cannot see what's happening or figure out which politicians to blame. The essential transaction would amount to misappropriating the trillions in Social Security taxes that workers have paid to finance their retirement benefits. This swindle is portrayed as "fiscal reform." In fact, it's the political equivalent of bait-and-switch fraud.

Defending Social Security sounds like yesterday's issue—the fight people won when they defeated George W. Bush's attempt to privatize the system in 2005. But the financial establishment has pushed it back on the table, claiming that the current crisis requires "responsible" leaders to take action. Will Obama take the bait? Surely not. The new president has been clear and consistent about Social Security, as a candidate and since his election. The program's financing is basically sound, he has explained, and can be assured far into the future by making only modest adjustments.

But Obama is also playing footsie with the conservative advocates of "entitlement reform" (their euphemism for cutting benefits). The president wants the corporate establishment's support on many other important matters, and he recently promised to hold a "fiscal responsibility summit" to examine the long-term costs of entitlements. That forum could set the trap for a "bipartisan compromise" that may become difficult for Obama to resist, given the burgeoning deficit. If he resists, he will be denounced as an old-fashioned free-spending liberal. The advocates are urging both parties to hold hands and take the leap together, authorizing big benefits cuts in a circuitous way that allows them to dodge the public's blame. In my new book, *Come Home, America*, I make the point: "When official America talks of 'bipartisan compromise,' it usually means the people are about to get screwed." ...

Higher Taxes on Workers

To understand the mechanics of this attempted swindle, you have to roll back twenty-five years, to the time the game of bait and switch began, under Ronald Reagan. The Gipper's great legislative victory in 1981—enacting massive tax cuts for corporations and upper-income ranks—launched the era of swollen federal budget deficits. But their economic impact was offset by the huge tax increase that Congress imposed on working people in 1983: the payroll tax rate supporting Social Security—the weekly FICA [Federal Insurance Contributions Act] deduction—was raised substantially, supposedly to create a nest egg for when the baby boom generation reached retirement age. A blue-ribbon commission chaired by [former chairman of the Federal Reserve Board] Alan Greenspan worked out the terms, then both parties signed on. Since there was no partisan fight, the press portrayed the massive tax increase as a noncontroversial "good government" reform.

Ever since, working Americans have paid higher taxes on their labor wages—12.4 percent, split between employees and employers. As a result, the Social Security system has accumulated a vast surplus—now around $2.5 trillion and growing. This is the money pot the establishment wants to grab, claiming the government can no longer afford to keep the promise it made to workers twenty-five years ago.

Actually, the government has already spent their money. Every year the Treasury has borrowed the surplus revenue collected by Social Security and spent the money on other purposes—whatever presidents and Congress decide, including more tax cuts for monied interests. The Social Security surplus thus makes the federal deficits seem smaller than they are—around $200 billion a year smaller. Each time the government dipped into the Social Security trust fund this way, it issued a legal obligation to pay back the money with interest whenever Social Security needed it to pay benefits.

Payback Time

That moment of reckoning is approaching. Uncle Sam owes these trillions to Social Security retirees and has to pay it back or look like just another deadbeat. That risk is the only "crisis" facing Social Security. It is the real reason powerful interests are so anxious to cut benefits. Social Security is not broke—not even close. It can sustain its obligations for roughly forty years, according to the Congressional Budget Office, even if nothing is changed. Even reports by the system's conservative trustees say it has no problem until 2041 (that report is signed by former Treasury Secretary Henry Paulson, the guy who bailed out the bankers). During the coming decade, however, the system will need to start drawing on its reserve surpluses to pay for benefits as boomers retire in greater numbers.

Peterson Attacks Social Security

Fifteen years ago [in 1992], Peter Peterson used some of the immense wealth he had accumulated as an investment banker to create and bankroll the Concord Coalition. The Concord Coalition was designed as a bipartisan organization promoting fiscal responsibility, with its primary targets being Social Security and Medicare. Peterson and his crew put out screeds, with titles like "Grey Dawn," that attacked these programs and warned that the growing wave of elderly would bankrupt the country.

Like most of the granny bashers, Peterson routinely played fast and loose with the facts.

Dean Baker, Alternet, October 16, 2007. www.alternet.org.

But if the government cuts the benefits first, it can push off repayment far into the future, and possibly forever. Otherwise, government has to borrow the money by selling government bonds or extend the Social Security tax to cover incomes above the current $107,000 ceiling. Obama endorses the latter option.

Follow the bouncing ball: Washington first cuts taxes on the well-to-do, then offsets the revenue loss by raising taxes on the working class and tells folks it is saving their money for future retirement. But Washington spends the money on other stuff, so when workers need it for their retirement, they are told, Sorry, we can't afford it.

Federal budget analysts try to brush aside these facts by claiming the government is merely "borrowing from itself" when it clips into Social Security. But that is a substantive falsehood. Government doesn't *own* this money. It essentially acts as the fiduciary, holding this wealth in trust for the "beneficial owners," the people who paid the taxes. This is the bait and switch the establishment intends to execute.

A Campaign of Fear

Peter Peterson, a Republican financier who made a fortune doing corporate takeover deals at Wall Street's Blackstone Group, is the Daddy Warbucks of the "fiscal responsibility" crusade. He has campaigned for decades against the dangers that old folks pose to the Republic. Now 82 and retired, Peterson claims he will spend nearly one-third of his $2.8 billion in wealth—he ranks 147 on the *Forbes* 400 list of richest Americans—alerting the public to this threat (leave aside the fact that old people have already paid for their retirement or that Social Security's modest benefits are equivalent to minimum-wage income). The major media treat him adoringly. Most reporters are too lazy (or dim) to check out the facts for themselves, so they simply repeat what Peterson tells them about Social Security.

It is a frightful message. Peterson describes a "$53 trillion hole" in America's fiscal condition—but the claim assumes numerous artful fallacies. His most blatant distortion is lumping Social Security, which is self-funded and sound, with other entitlements like Medicare and Medicaid. Those programs do face financial crisis. . . .

Peterson's proposal would essentially dismantle the Social Security entitlement enacted in the New Deal, much as [former President] Bill Clinton repealed the right to welfare. Peterson has assembled influential allies for this radical step. They include a coalition of six major think tanks and four tax-exempt foundations.

Their report—*Taking Back Our Fiscal Future*, issued jointly by [the think tanks] the Brookings Institution and the Heritage Foundation—recommends that Congress put long-term budget caps on Social Security and other entitlement spending, which would automatically trigger benefits cuts if needed to stay within the prescribed limits. The same antidemocratic mechanisms—a commission of technocrats and limited Congressional discretion—would shield politicians from popular blowback. . . .

Provoking Conflict

The ugliest ploy in their campaign is the effort to provoke conflict between the generations. "The automatic funding of Social Security, Medicare and Medicaid impedes explicit consideration of competing priorities and threatens to squeeze out spending for young people," these economists declared. Children, it is suggested, are being shortchanged by their grandparents. This line of argument has attracted financial support from some leading foundations usually associated with liberal social concerns—Annie E. Casey, Charles Stewart Mott, William and Flora Hewlett. Peterson has teamed up with the Pew Trust and has also created front groups of "concerned youth."

Trouble is, most young people did not buy this pitch when George W. Bush used it to sell Social Security privatization. Most kids seem to think Grandma is entitled to a decent retirement. In fact, whacking Social Security benefits, not to mention Medicaid, directly harms poor children. More poor children live in families dependent on Social Security checks than on welfare, economist Dean Baker points out. If you cut Grandma's Social Security benefits, you are directly making life worse for the poor kids who live with her.

The assault sounds outrageous and bound to fail, but the conservative interests may have Obama in a neat trap. Their fog of scary propaganda makes it easier to distort the president's position and blame him for any fiscal disorders driven by the current financial collapse. He will be urged to "do the right thing" for the country and make the hard choices, regardless of petty political grievances (words and phrases he has used himself). Obama's fate may depend on informing the public—now, not later—so that people are inoculated against these artful lies.

A Real Solution

The real crisis, in any case, is not Social Security but the colossal failure of the private pension system. Most people know this, either because their 401(k) account is pitifully inadequate, or their company dumped its pension plan, or the plummeting stock market devoured their savings. Obama can protect himself with the public by speaking candidly about this reality and proposing a forceful, long-term solution. He should expand the guarantees that ordinary people need to get their families through these adverse times. Instead of taking away old promises to people, the president should make some new ones. Healthcare reform is obviously an important imperative, but so is retirement security.

The solution to retirement insecurity is the creation of a national pension, alongside Social Security, that would be the bedrock social insurance. Improving Social Security benefits is one step, but it cannot possibly restore what so many middle-class families have lost. Tinkering with the 401(k) would be doomed, because it is basically a tax subsidy for the middle and upper classes, another way to avoid taxes that failed utterly to produce real savings.

The new universal pension would be mainly self-financing—that is, funded by mandatory savings—but the system would operate as a government-supervised nonprofit, not manipulated by corporate executives or Wall Street firms. A national pension would combine the best qualities of defined-benefit plans and individual accounts. Each worker's pension would be individualized and portable, moving with job changes, but the savings would be pooled with others for diversified investment.

There is nothing radical about this approach. It follows the form of the government's thrift savings plan for civil servants and members of Congress, TIAA-CREF for college professors or other union pension plans jointly managed by labor and management trustees. The crucial difference is that since the new universal pension would be nonprofit, nobody would get to play self-interested games with the money that employees are storing in it for retirement.

> *"As the identity of the pivotal voter changes—and the median voter becomes older—the political support for social security increases."*

The Politics of an Aging Population Make Social Security Cuts Difficult

Vincenzo Galasso

Vincenzo Galasso is a professor at Bocconi University in Milan, Italy. In the viewpoint that follows, Galasso argues that the aging of developed societies makes generous pension systems economically unsustainable. However, the same demographic trend makes it difficult for policy-makers to cut social security benefits or eligibility—policies he calls "retrenchment." Nevertheless, Galasso predicts that voters will opt for raising the retirement age because they realize that a large number of pensioners actually threatens to reduce pension system payouts.

As you read, consider the following questions:

1. According to forecasts, what percentage of the developed world's population will be elderly in 2050, according to Galasso?

Vincenzo Galasso, *The Political Future of Social Security in Aging Societies.* Cambridge, Mass.: MIT Press, 2006. Copyright © 2006 Massachusetts Institute of Technology. All rights reserved. Reproduced by permission.

2. How did pensions policy change in European countries in the 1980s and 1990s, in the author's view?

3. Why does Galasso say that Spain is expected to have one of the largest increases in pension spending?

The world population is aging fast. In 2000 individuals aged 65 years or more represented about 7 percent of the world population, up from 5.2 percent in 1950. Yet United Nations projections suggest that this share of the aged will double to reach 16 percent in 2050. The population aging is even more pronounced if one considers only the more developed regions of the world. The fraction of elderly individuals—those aged 65 years or more—in Europe, Northern America, Australia, New Zealand, and Japan has already increased from 8 percent in 1950 to 14 percent in 2000, and is forecasted to reach 26 percent in 2050.

This dramatic demographic dynamics is the result of a contemporaneous drop in mortality and fertility rates. The reduction in mortality seems to represent a long-lasting trend, which has already generated substantial longevity gains during the last fifty years. UN data indicate an increase in the average world life expectancy at birth from 46.5 years in 1950 to 65.4 years in 2000, yet further longevity gains are forecasted, with the average life expectancy reaching 74.3 years by 2050. Also the drop in fertility seems to follow a trend, although in the more developed countries the large fall in the number of births has mainly occurred during the eighties and nineties and is now expected to stabilize. According to these forecasted demographic dynamics, aging will hence continue.

Implications of Aging Populations

Population aging bears significant implications for the economic environment. The structure of production may have to adjust to accommodate a labor force with a different age composition. Individuals may respond to their increased longevity by saving more for old age consumption, thereby leading to higher aggregate savings and to a larger stock of physical capital. The composition of the aggregate demand may also change, since a graying society will express different needs, and presumably higher demand for goods and services for the old, such as recreational entertainment and long-term care. The relative importance of the different schemes in the welfare state will also be affected, with more emphasis being [put] on programs targeted to the elderly, such as social security, health insurance, and long-term care.

Aging has also dramatic consequences for the functioning of unfunded, or pay-as-you-go (PAYG), social security systems. In an unfunded system, contributions imposed on the labor earnings of covered workers are used to provide pension benefits to current retirees. Thus aging has a direct impact on the financial solvency of social security, since it tends to increase the fraction of recipients—the retirees—while reducing the proportion of contributors—the workers. To restore the financial balance of the system, either pension benefits have to be reduced or the tax burden on the workers has to be increased. The magnitude of this phenomenon is captured by the changes in the old age dependency ratio, which is defined as the ratio of elderly (aged 65 years or more) to adult individuals (aged between 18 and 64 years). In Italy and Spain this ratio is projected to double in less than fifty years, increasing respectively from 27.9 and 26 percent in 2000 to 64.5 and 63.5 percent in 2050. Together with these changes in the age composition of the population, most OECD [Organization for Economic Cooperation and Development] countries have also experienced a large drop in the labor force participation of middle-aged and elderly workers. These early exits from the labor market, which were induced by the introduction—since the late sixties—of generous early retirement schemes, have further increased the number of retirees— hence contributing financial distress to the systems.

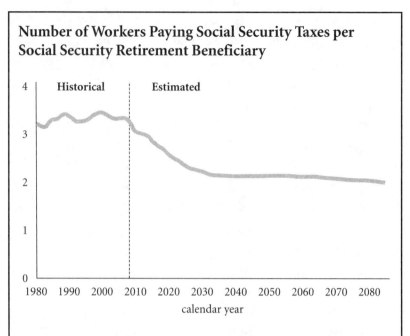

Number of Workers Paying Social Security Taxes per Social Security Retirement Beneficiary

TAKEN FROM: Jason J. Fichtner et al., Annual Report of the Board of Trustees of the Federal Old-Age and Survivors Insurance and Federal Disability Insurance Trust Funds. Washington D.C.: Government Printing Office, 2009.

A Scramble to Reform Pensions

The scale of population aging, and its dramatic effects on the unfunded pension systems, have captured the attention of economists, media, and policy-makers—giving rise in several European countries to a flurry of pension reforms. During the eighties and nineties, in fact, incremental policies that extended the coverage and generosity of the welfare state were progressively abandoned, while mild retrenching measures were instead adopted. Most reforms amounted only to moderate variations in the parameters of the systems, which did not modify their underlying unfunded nature or defined benefit structure. Yet sometimes these conservative changes to the benefit calculation criteria, to the eligibility requirements, to the indexation rule, and particularly to the effective retirement age managed to reduce the generosity of these systems—often along a lengthy transition period—and thus to enhance their long-term financial sustainability. To summarize these different scenarios, EU [European Union] official projections on the future financial sustainability of European social security systems forecast changes in pension expenditure for the next fifty years to range between a small reduction in the United Kingdom—from 5.1 percent of GDP [gross domestic product] in 2000 to 3.9 percent in 2050—and a large increase in Spain—from 9.4 to 17.7 percent, depending on the different magnitude of the aging process, of the initial status quo and of the reforming experience of the last decades.

These calculations, however accurate, fail to consider that the design, the rules or the crucial parameters of the social security systems may further be modified. For instance, will the legislated—but yet to be introduced—retrenching measures ever be implemented? Or will policy-makers decide to renege on reforms adopted by previous governments—as in Germany during the nineties—and thus to stop their phasing in? In other words, how will further aging affect the development of these unfunded pension systems?

Conventional economic wisdom suggests that further aging will require additional retrenchment efforts to limit the growth of pension spending. Indeed, even if per-capita pension benefits are reduced, aggregate pension spending—and hence social security contributions—is still likely to rise, due to the increasing proportion of retirees. Yet, unlike welfare state expansion measures, retrenchment policies are extremely unpopular. Welfare states enjoy extended support among pensions' recipients and bureaucrats, who strongly oppose any benefit reduction. Electoral concerns—and political pressure by unions and lobby groups—may thus dictate the social security policy decisions of policy-makers, who face a political plea not to retrench....

Curtailing Benefits Unpopular

The extension of the coverage and the rise in the pension benefits' generosity that characterized the growth in social spending since World War II are popular measures that typically generate positive electoral returns. The politics of welfare state retrenchment is instead an exercise in electoral blame avoidance—since retrenching measures tend to impose large costs on specific groups of voters, while creating only dispersed and uncertain gains. Exploiting external constraints to reduce the political accountability of these policies or adopting "divide-and-rule" strategies may help to minimize electoral backslashes, but the relevance of electoral concerns remains crucial.

An analysis of the political sustainability of social security under aging thus needs to examine the individuals' position on social security issues in order to assess the political relevance of these vested interests. Preferences over social security typically depend on an individual's age—since different cohorts [groups] of people face different remaining periods of contributions and benefits, but also on the redistributive design of the system. Retirees who receive a pension benefit at no current cost, middle-aged individuals who consider past contributions to the system as a sunk cost, or low income young individuals who benefit from within cohort redistribution may experience an increase in their economic well-being, thanks to social security. These individuals, who represent the constituency of the welfare state, will thus oppose retrenchment, and their electoral push may lead policy-makers to refrain from reforming the system. . . .

Support Grows as Society Ages

The aging society hands over to the policy-maker a crucial trade-off between economic efficiency and political accountability. In fact demographic dynamics affect the individuals' preferences over social security—through changes in the average return from the pension system—but also the political process—through the aging of the electorate. In an environment with a stable employment the average internal rate of return of a PAYG social security system is equal to the sum of the population and the productivity growth rate. Yet individual returns are also affected by the survival probabilities that determine the length of the retirement period. Aging thus reduces the average return, although longevity gains may dampen this effect, and should induce the agents to reduce their support for social security. In the political arena, however, the aging society augments the political relevance of the elderly voters—those close to retirement. As the identity of the pivotal voter changes—and the median [age of the] voter becomes older—the political support for social security increases.

The impact of the demographic process on the long run political sustainability of social security depends also on some characteristic features of the system. For instance, pension schemes enabling massive early retirements, as in France and Italy, amplify the negative impact of aging on the average profitability of the system, since the growing share of middle-aged individuals will be induced to retire early rather than continue to contribute to the system, while countries with high pension spending, such as Italy, may already experience too severe economic distortions because of the large social security contribution rate. . . .

Under population aging the political push—corresponding to the aging electorate—is forecasted to dominate the economic elements—consisting of the reduction in the average profitability of the system. Pension spending is estimated to rise sharply in all six countries. . . . The largest increases are expected to occur in Spain, the fastest aging country, but also in the United Kingdom, with contribution rates rising respectively from 21.3 and 14.5 percent in 2000 to 45.5 and 33.2 percent in 2050. Yet Italy would still experience the largest contribution rate, 50 percent. These significant rises in the social security contribution rate, and thus in the overall pension spending, would nevertheless be accompanied by some retrenching measures, with pension benefits' generosity falling—in France, Germany, Italy, and Spain. In the United Kingdom and the United States, higher social security contribution rates would instead be associated with more generous pensions. . . .

A Possible Solution

Postponing retirement represents an effective measure to limit the increase in pension spending induced by population aging—as measured by the social security contribution rate—while typically increasing the generosity of the system. The intuition is straightforward. A rise in the effective retirement age moderates the political demand for more social security, since it reduces the expected retirement period, while increasing the contribution period for the decisive voter. This policy measure is particularly successful in those countries with a low initial effective retirement age, such as France and Italy, in which a rise in the retirement age to 65 years would reduce contributions by around 12 percent. In all other countries the effect would be smaller, but still sizable.

However, is this policy measure politically feasible? Would individuals be willing to work longer years? Simulations on the political support to postponing retirement give an encouraging picture. In all countries a majority of voters is expected to support an increase in the retirement age. In fact aging tends to decrease the individual's lifetime income—due to the presence of a large social security system whose profitability will largely drop—while lower pension benefits will reduce the incentives to retire early. These two effects will hence induce the electors to postpone retirement.

> *"The days when defined benefit pensions were a major support of American retirement systems are over."*

Private Pensions Are Failing to Provide Retirement Security

Charles R. Morris

Charles R. Morris is an investment banker and financial writer whose most recent book is The Tycoons. *In the following viewpoint he makes the case that the United States' reliance on private pensions endangers many Americans' prospects for a financially secure retirement. A significant number of employer-funded retirement programs are in serious financial difficulty—workers can no longer depend on them. Moreover, the rate of participation in tax-advantaged individual retirement accounts (IRAs) is low, especially among those with lower incomes. Morris warns that the baby boom generation will reach retirement age without an adequate pension system in place.*

Charles R. Morris, *Apart at the Seams: The Collapse of Private Pension and Health Care Protections.* New York: Century Foundation Press, 2006. Copyright © 2006 The Century Foundation, Inc. All rights reserved. Reproduced by permission.

As you read, consider the following questions:

1. According to the author, what percentage of gross domestic product does the United States spend on social insurance such as retirement and health insurance programs?

2. In dollar amounts, how did corporate pensions fund positions change from 1999 to 2005, according to Morris?

3. According to an estimate derived from 1997 tax returns, as cited by the author, what percentage of the population contributes to tax-advantaged individual retirement accounts such as 401(k)s?

Retirement and health provision in the United States are built around four primary programs. Two of them are federal: Social Security—officially, Old-Age, Survivors, and Disability Insurance (OASDI)—and Medicare/Medicaid. Medicare and Medicaid are aimed at different target populations, but there are many overlaps, most notably in the financing of nursing home and home health care for seniors. The second two are the private sector, employer-sponsored, retirement and health insurance systems. Since the categorical restrictions on the federal programs exclude most working-age people and their families, the majority of Americans rely on employer-sponsored benefits in the welfare capitalist tradition.

American Social Insurance

The four primary programs account for the dominant portion of what analysts call American "social insurance"—which would also include food stamps, unemployment compensation, the earned income tax credit, and similar programs. Perhaps surprisingly, within the recent past, the total social insurance provision as a share of U.S. GDP [gross domestic product] has been roughly at the norm for other major industrial countries. OECD [Organization for Economic Cooperation and Development] economists have analyzed total social insurance spending in major countries, using 1995 data, including both public and "private social" spending. ("Private social" spending is managed by nonpublic entities, such as employers, but is regulated or subsidized through favorable taxation or other measures.) The spending calculations also include "tax expenditures" such as employer tax deductions for worker benefits. (The value of federal tax expenditures for private sector pensions and health insurance is estimated at more than $250 billion in 2005, or nearly as much as the total Medicare budget.) Over the sample of thirteen countries, the share of GDP dedicated to social insurance spending was tightly clustered, consuming about a quarter of national resources everywhere, despite considerable variation in financing and taxation mechanisms.

The United States, with 24.5 percent of its GDP devoted to social insurance, according to the OECD analysts, was exactly in the median position of the countries in the sample. The top spender in the sample, Germany, devoted 27.7 percent of GDP to social insurance, so the gap between the median and top position was modest.

The question, then, is why are there are such gaping holes in the American social insurance system? Why do so many workers have only minimal protection for retirement income and, often, no health care coverage at all. The answer, in part, is because the United States relies to such a great extent on its crumbling "private social" system. The share of private social provision in U.S. social insurance is more than twice as high as in the next highest country, and more than four times the median. . . .

Defined Benefit Pensions

To the Depression-era generation entering the workforce after World War II, one of the secrets of the good life was to catch on with "a big company with a pension." Although fewer than half of private sector workers ever had a defined benefit pension, it was one of the trademark features of the American dream—a defined benefit pension, promising a set monthly payment for the rest of your life, and usually your spouse's life, so long as you put in the service time. The first realization that pension promises were not ironclad may have come when the Studebaker Co. folded in 1963 and defaulted on its pension obligations. Congress eventually responded with the Employee Retirement Income Security Act (ERISA) of 1974. ERISA established financing and accounting standards for defined benefit pensions and created the federal Pension Benefit Guarantee Corporation (PBGC) to insure private defined benefit pension commitments.

The modern portfolio management industry is, to a great extent, a creature of ERISA's requirement that companies set aside assets to fund their future pension liabilities. If the actuarially [by insurance statistics] determined present value of pension liabilities exceeds that of pension fund assets, the shortfall is subtracted from the company's net worth as if it were a debt. As of mid-2005, private companies have amassed $1.8 trillion in assets to support their defined benefit pension obligations, against future liabilities valued at about $2.2 trillion. Pension funds initially concentrated their investments in high-grade bond portfolios, but as the stock market recovered through the 1980s, funds gradually shifted to higher-yielding stocks, in the hope that higher returns would allow reductions in annual contributions. During the 1990s market boom, stock returns were so high that many plans became overfunded, and pension funds actually became an important driver of company earnings. When the markets reversed after 2000, pension fund underperformance hammered profits, at the same time as falling operating earnings reduced companies' ability to increase plan contributions. Just as important, although not

Waning Health Benefits

Most Americans have health insurance through their employers, yet employment is no longer a guarantee of health insurance coverage. As America continues to move from a manufacturing-based economy to a service economy, and employee working patterns continue to evolve, health insurance coverage has become less stable. The service sector offers less access to health insurance than its manufacturing counterparts.

Due to rising health insurance premiums, many small employers cannot afford to offer health benefits. Companies that do offer health insurance, often require employees to contribute a larger share toward their coverage. As a result, an increasing number of Americans have opted not to take advantage of job-based health insurance because they cannot afford it.

National Coalition on Health Care, July 2009.

widely understood, the steady fall in interest rates after 2001 greatly ratcheted up the book value of future pension liabilities.

Funding Deficits

The negative swing in corporate pension fund positions has been roughly $750 billion since 1999—from a $300 billion surplus plus to an estimated $450 billion deficit as of mid-2005. Analysts at CreditSuisse/First Boston (CSFB) recently published a list of twenty major companies with pension liabilities that equal or exceed the company's market value; the list includes Delta Airlines (which has since declared bankruptcy), with pension obligations 13 times higher than its market value; General Motors, 4.7 times higher; Ford, 2.7

times higher; Lucent, 1.9 times higher; and U.S. Steel, 1.4 times higher. Mounting deficits at the PBGC are creating the potential for a federal bailout on the scale of the 1980s Savings and Loan crisis. (Technically, the PBGC, which is supposed to be self-financing through fees and insurance premiums, has no legal call on the federal purse, but political pressure for a federal response could be overwhelming.)

A number of proposals are being floated to shore up defined benefit pension funding and accounting, but most would require companies to report higher levels of debt and lower profits. More likely, companies will accelerate the process of extracting themselves from their pension obligations. One path is the strategic bankruptcy. Shedding pension obligations has become practically a standardized financial engineering tool in the hands of private equity buyout managers—in steel companies, auto parts companies, and more recently, a string of airline bankruptcies. . . .

Less dramatic alternatives include terminating a plan, or closing it to new employees, or converting it to a "cash balance" plan.[1] Even financially healthy companies, like IBM, have been taking the cash balance route; at least a third of employees in nominally "defined benefit" pension plans have been converted to the cash balance format.

In short, the days when defined benefit pensions were a major support of American retirement systems are over. Currently, only about 20 percent of private sector workers participate in defined benefit pensions, and that number will drop to the vanishing point over the next ten years or so. Overall, defined benefit coverage is higher because almost all federal employees and up to 90 percent of state and local government employees are members of defined benefit plans. Analysts have estimated, however, that the unfunded liabilities of state and local defined benefit plans are even higher than in the

1. A cash balance account is an employer-sponsored individual savings account to which the employer and employee contribute.

private sector. Pension fund payments have become the fastest-growing items in many jurisdictions, squeezing out education and other essential spending. State issues of tens of billions of "pension obligation bonds" to take advantage of rising markets in the late 1990s have only worsened the problem. The phasing in of private-sector-like accounting rules for state and local governments starting in the late 1990s is forcing accurate disclosure, although their initial effects have been masked by superb market returns—indeed, many jurisdictions fattened benefits. "Smoothing" provisions have also blunted the stated impact of market underperformance and falling discount rates, but the scale of the liability overhang cannot be suppressed much longer.

Defined Contribution Pensions

Defined contribution pensions—primarily 401(k) plans—are employer-sponsored tax-advantaged savings and investment accounts under the control of the covered employee. Maximum contributions in any year are up to 20 percent of salary, not to exceed $14,000 at present [2006]. Labor Department survey data show that 53 percent of private sector employees had access to a defined contribution plan in 2004, and 42 percent actually participated in a plan. In about 80 percent of the defined contribution plans, the employer makes some form of a matching contribution. Total defined contribution pension assets in mid-2005, at some $2.7 trillion, are about 50 percent greater than defined benefit plan assets.

A major advantage of defined contribution plans is that, unlike defined benefit pensions, they are portable—when an employee leaves a firm, the defined contribution account goes with her. Vesting rules usually apply to the employer's contribution, although they are typically more lenient than those for defined benefit plans. During the initial proliferation of defined contribution plans, they were often badly abused by employers—by requiring employees to invest their accounts in the sponsoring company stock, for example. Current rules have eliminated the worst abuses and ensure that employees are offered a reasonable menu of investment alternatives. Companies are realizing as well that most employees need advice on basic investment strategies: left to their own devices, many merely concentrate their funds in cash-like accounts, forgoing the opportunities for compounded returns.

The primary problem with defined contribution pensions—even leaving aside the more than half of all private sector workers who have *neither* a defined benefit or a defined contribution plan—is the paltriness of the coverage built up by the average worker. A Census Bureau survey of household asset holdings in 2000 showed that the middle-quintile [middle-fifth] income household, with a middle-aged household head (45–54), had net financial assets of just $12,725, plus $43,917 of home equity. Among all middle-quintile households, only a quarter held any 401(k) or other thrift-type asset, fewer than 20 percent had IRAs or similar instruments (in the lowest quintile, fewer than 9 percent), and even fewer held any stocks or mutual funds other than those in their retirement accounts. Earners in the two lower quintiles, for all practical purposes, had almost no retirement savings at all.

Low Participation Rates

A study by the Congressional Budget Office teased out participation rates in tax-advantaged programs from 1997 tax returns. The study uses different income categories from the Census Bureau's and, because of the nature of the data, did not break out private sector employees. Among all income groups, however, only 27 percent participated in 401(k) or similar plans. Participation among the low earners was only 6 percent, rising to more than 50 percent in households earning more than $80,000. Not surprisingly, only 1 percent of the low-earning households with 401(k)s made any contributions in the year surveyed; but strikingly, in households earning between $40,000 and $80,000, only 4 percent made the maximum contribution: Even worse, one recent survey showed that 45 percent of workers—and 42 percent of workers aged 40–49—withdrew all their plan contributions when they changed jobs. The rate of participation in IRAs and other nonemployment-based savings programs is even lower: a risible [laughable] 6 percent of all earners—2 percent in the low-earning households and 17 percent among the top earners (above $160,000). Total IRA assets, however, at $3.4 trillion are nearly triple the assets in defined benefit pension funds and about a quarter larger than defined contribution pension assets. Ownership of those assets obviously is skewed toward the upper-income quintiles. . . .

In the final analysis, however, the retirement finance problem is probably not nearly as serious as the health care financing challenge. Some academic economists, indeed, suspect that the retirement savings issue is being exaggerated by the fund management industry. One study, for example, based on results from a representative panel of people born between 1931 and 1941, finds that 80 percent of the panel had either adequate savings, or more than they needed. Average shortfalls of the undersavers, moreover, were not large. A key point was that for the poorest third of the cohort [statistical group], who generally had little or no savings, Social Security income was sufficient for their needs—which is consistent with the low rate of poverty among the elderly, and a long-term trend toward earlier retirement. An important concern is whether the recent collapse in household savings especially if it is accompanied by a flattening or downturn in house prices, will generate significantly different outcomes for the next cohorts of retirees. This is clearly an area where there is a pressing need for continued, empirical, policy-related research. . . .

Pension Problems Will Worsen

All four of the basic pillars of the American social insurance system are in serious difficulty: despite its well-publicized problems, Social Security is arguably in the best shape of all. The promise of "golden-age" welfare capitalism to see to the retirement income and health care needs of its workers has clearly broken down. There are serious questions about whether American workers are acquiring adequate resources for retirement, and the day is approaching when only a minority of employers will offer health insurance at all. And these problems are all on the cusp of becoming *much* worse as the baby-boom generation becomes a massive consumer of retirement and health care resources.

Periodical Bibliography

The following articles have been selected to supplement the diverse views presented in this chapter.

Jonathan Chait	"Fact Finders," *New Republic*, February 2, 2005.
Larry DeWitt	"Financing Social Security, 1939–1949: A Reexamination of the Financing Policies of This Period," *Social Security Bulletin*, December, 2007.
GAO Reports	"The Nation's Long-Term Fiscal Outlook," May 16, 2008. www.gao.gov.
James K. Glassman and Tyler Cowen	"The Death of Social Security," *Reason*, April 2005.
Savannah Schroll Guz	"Social Security: A Documentary History," *Library Journal*, March 1, 2008.
Teresa T. King and H. Wayne Cecil	"The History of Major Changes to the Social Security System," *CPA Journal*, May 2006.
Brian McCabe	"Preserving Social Security for Future Generations," *Saturday Evening Post*, May/June 2005.
Joseph A. McCartin	"Social Security: History and Politics from the New Deal to the Privatization Debate," *American Historical Review*, December 2006.
Charles R. Morris	"Just the Facts," *Commonweal*, February 11, 2005.
Doug Orr	"Revisiting the 'Dependency Ratio,'" *Dollars & Sense*, March/April 2005.
Doug Orr	"Social Security Q&A," *Dollars & Sense*, May/June 2005.
Pat Regnier and Carolyn Bigda	"What Every Family Needs to Know About Social Security," *Money*, April 2005.

OPPOSING
VIEWPOINTS®
SERIES

CHAPTER 2

How Should the Social Security System Be Reformed?

Chapter Preface

While there are a variety of opinions on the severity of the problems with Social Security, there is a consensus among both liberals and conservatives that some change in the system will be required. There is, however, a great deal of disagreement as to what changes will be necessary. In general, conservatives favor the privatization of retirement accounts, while liberals favor adjustments to improve the current system.

Plans for privatization of Social Security usually call for the abolition of the current system of payroll taxes. Currently about 12.6 percent of an individual's wages are paid into the system, half by the employee and half directly by the employer. Under privatization, individuals would keep this 12.6 percent on the condition that it be invested in a private retirement account. Advocates of this approach believe that individuals who supervise their own investments will get a better return in the long run than they would receive from the current pay-as-you-go (PAYGO) system. Moreover, these investments would lead to greater economic growth, they believe. Privatization advocate professor Martin Feldstein of Harvard University projected in the late 1990s that "the combination of the improved labor market incentives and the higher real return on savings has a net present value gain of more than $15 trillion, an amount equivalent to 3 percent of each future year's GDP [gross domestic product] forever."

Privatized retirement systems have their critics. They often point to Chile, which privatized its social security system in 1981. While investment returns for most individuals in the system have been good—averaging about 10 percent per year from the program's start until 2005—about half of Chilean workers do not participate because they are self-employed or work irregular jobs. Moreover, average returns do not reflect how individuals fare; some saw their retirement portfolios stagnate. In 2005 the *New York Times* related the plight of laboratory technician Dagoberto Sáez, whose private investments left him with much less retirement income than those who stayed with Chile's old, state-backed system.

"Colleagues and friends with the same pay grade who stayed in the old system, people who work right alongside me," he said, "are retiring with pensions of almost $700 a month—good until they die. I have a salary that allows me to live with dignity, and all of a sudden I am going to be plunged into poverty, all because I made the mistake of believing the promises they made to us back in 1981."

The last major call for Social Security privatization was issued by Republican president George W. Bush in his State of the Union address of 2005. His proposals did not succeed. Because of President Barack Obama's return of the White House to the Democrats—the more liberal of the U.S. political parties—and perhaps even more because of volatility in the stock and bond markets in the late 2000s, privatization of the nation's retirement system in the near future seems doubtful. Even Chile, the first country to put individual retirement accounts at the center of its retirement system, has instituted reform; the government now supplements the private accounts with a state pension.

Even though privatization now appears to be dead, or at least in hibernation, the United States Social Security system continues to face real difficulties. The imminent retirement of the baby boomers, the large generation of Americans, born between 1946 and 1964, means that more retirees will be relying on fewer workers for their retirement check. In the following chapter's viewpoints, the authors debate how to meet this challenge.

> "[Social Security's] projected deficit is small enough that it can be eliminated through a progressive reform that combines modest benefit reductions and revenue increases."

Increased Taxes and Reduced Benefits Can Strengthen Social Security

Peter A. Diamond and Peter R. Orszag

Peter A. Diamond is a professor of economics at the Massachusetts Institute of Technology. Peter R. Orszag is director of the Office of Management and Budget in the Barack Obama administration.

To save Social Security, the authors in the following viewpoint argue that it is necessary to increase the maximum "cap" on wages subject to payroll tax. (In 2009 any amount over $106,800 was free of payroll tax.) They aim to have 13 percent of wages free of payroll tax, versus the 15 percent that escapes the tax today. A gradual increase in the overall rate of payroll tax, as well as a gradual reduction in benefits also figure in their plan. The authors contend that their straightforward plan can

Peter A. Diamond and Peter R. Orszag, "Saving Social Security: The Diamond Orszag Plan," *The Economists' Voice*, vol. 2, no. 1, 2005, pp. 1–7. Copyright © Peter A. Diamond and Peter R. Orszag. Reproduced by permission.

*save Social Security, and that dramatic upheavals, such as re-
placing the system with private individual accounts, would only
cause further harm.*

As you read, consider the following questions:

1. How has the proportion of total earnings above the taxable maximum changed in the last two decades, according to the authors?

2. What is the "legacy debt," and how does it effect Social
   Security, in Diamond and Orszag's opinion?

3. What would the payroll tax rate be in 2035 under the
   authors' plan?

Social Security is one of America's most successful government programs. It has helped millions of Americans avoid
poverty in old age, upon becoming disabled, or after the death
of a family wage earner. To be sure, the program faces a long-
term deficit and is in need of updating. But Social Security's
long-term financial health can be restored through modest adjustments. Major surgery is neither warranted nor desirable,
in our view.

Over the next 75 years, the actuarial [statistically calcu-
lated] deficit in Social Security amounts to 0.7 percent of
Gross Domestic Product (GDP); projected out forever, the
deficit is 1.2 percent of GDP. (Most of the time you will see
Social Security benefits measured as percentages of "taxable
payroll"—the base of Social Security taxes. "Taxable payroll" is
roughly 40 percent of GDP, so deficit numbers as a percentage
of taxable payroll are roughly 2[frac12] times deficits as percentages of GDP.) The important thing is that this projected
deficit is small enough that it can be eliminated through a
progressive reform that combines modest benefit reductions
and revenue increases. In this article we will explain briefly
how that can be done. . . .

Painful Choices

The Social Security deficit can be eliminated only through different combinations of politically painful choices: tax increases and benefit reductions. Unfortunately, too many analysts and politicians have ignored this reality, responding to the painful alternatives by embracing "free lunch" approaches.

Some unrealistically assume trillions of dollars will be transferred from the rest of the budget to Social Security, despite substantial deficits projected in that part of the budget. Others would let Social Security borrow trillions to finance investment in stocks, playing off the difference in expected returns between stocks and Treasury bonds—but without taking risk into account.

Yet avoiding real reform, either through delay or a free lunch approach, merely exacerbates the painful choices that will ultimately be necessary. Even those who disagree with the specifics of our plan should agree that it is gimmick-free; unfortunately, too few other plans meet this relatively low standard.

Our plan makes the painful choices that are necessary—selecting a combination of benefit and revenue changes to restore long-term balance. In doing so, it focuses on three areas which contribute to the actuarial imbalance: improvements in life expectancy, increases in earnings inequality, and the burden of the legacy debt from Social Security's early history.

An Increasing Life Expectancy

The first area is increasing life expectancy. Since 1940, life expectancy at age 65 has increased by four years for men and five for women, and is expected to continue rising. And of course, further years of life means further years of Social Security payments.

To offset the cost from further increases in life expectancy, we propose a balanced combination of benefit reductions and tax increases. Specifically, in each year the Office of the Chief

Taxing Inheritances

Relative to unspecified general revenue transfers to Social Security, an estate tax or inheritance tax is attractive because it could be used as a dedicated source of funds. The revenue collected under the tax is explicit; no estimation or projection is necessary. Moreover, dedicating estate or inheritance tax revenue to Social Security would support the important tradition of keeping Social Security out of the annual budget discussion. Given that so many Americans rely so much on Social Security, its provisions should be adjusted only from time to time, not every year, and with lead times to help workers adapt. The idea of using an estate tax to finance benefits for elderly persons and disabled workers is not new. Indeed, it is over 200 years old, Thomas Paine having proposed it in 1797.

Peter A. Diamond and Peter R. Orszag,
Saving Social Security: A Balanced Approach, *2005.*

Actuary would calculate the net cost to Social Security from the improvement in life expectancy. Half of this cost would be offset by a reduction in benefits, which would apply to all workers age 59 and younger. The other half would be financed by an increase in the payroll tax rate.

Implementing this proposal would reduce the seventy-five-year actuarial deficit by 0.55 percent of taxable payroll, slightly less than a third of the currently projected deficit.

Increasing Earnings Inequality

Social Security's financing is affected by two recent trends: the increase in the share of earnings that are above the maximum taxable earnings base ($90,000 in 2005) and are therefore untaxed, and the widening of the difference in life expectancy between lower earners and higher earners.

Over the past two decades, the fraction of aggregate earnings above the taxable maximum has risen from 10 to 15 percent. Our plan gradually raises the taxable maximum, so that the percentage of aggregate earnings above it returns about halfway to its 1983 level—that is, to 13 percent—by 2063. (This raises the payroll tax for roughly six percent of workers each year, those with the highest earnings, and raises the marginal tax rate for even fewer workers.)

Furthermore, people with higher earnings and more education are increasingly tending to live longer than less-educated, lower-earning workers. This hurts Social Security finances and reduces progressiveness on a lifetime basis, since the highest earners receive payments over an increasingly longer period compared to everyone else. To offset this trend, our plan would gradually reduce the highest tier of the benefit formula, affecting the 15 percent of workers with the highest lifetime earnings.

These two changes would reduce the seventy-five-year actuarial deficit by 0.43 percent of taxable payroll.

Confronting the Legacy Debt

Third, and finally, our plan addresses the burden of the legacy debt. Benefits paid to almost all current and past cohorts [statistical groups] of beneficiaries exceeded what could have been financed with the revenue they contributed. This difference is what we call the legacy debt. Without this debt—that is, if earlier cohorts had received only the benefits that could be financed by their contributions plus interest, the trust fund's assets today would be much greater. Those assets would earn interest, which could be used to finance benefits.

We cannot take back the benefits that were given to Social Security's early beneficiaries, and most Americans seem unwilling to reduce benefits for those now receiving them, or soon to receive them. Those two facts largely determine the size of the legacy debt.

The key issue is how to finance this legacy debt across different generations, and across different people within generations. We propose three changes that contribute to restoring balance and represent an allocation of the financing of the program's legacy debt:

First, mandate Social Security coverage for newly hired state and local government workers, so that eventually all workers will bear their fair share of the cost of the nation's earlier generosity.

Second, create a legacy tax on earnings above the maximum taxable earnings base, so that very high earners contribute to financing the legacy debt in proportion to their full earnings. This legacy tax would start at 3.0 percent and increase along with the universal charge, described next.

Third, create a universal legacy charge. Roughly half will appear as a benefit reduction for all beneficiaries becoming eligible in or after 2023. The rest will appear as an increase in the payroll tax from 2023 onward. These charges, together, will gradually increase, in order to help stabilize the ratio of the legacy debt to taxable payroll.

These three approaches to the legacy debt issue would reduce the seventy-five-year actuarial deficit by 0.19, 0.55, and 0.97 percent of taxable payroll respectively.

Our three-part proposal would restore seventy-five-year actuarial balance and ensure that the trust fund is slightly rising relative to expenditures at the end of 75 years. It also provides sufficient resources to finance targeted improvements for widows, workers with low earnings over a long career, workers disabled at young ages, and young surviving children.

Effects on Benefits and Taxes

What do these various changes imply for the benefits that workers will receive, and for the taxes they will pay?

Workers who are 55 or older will experience no change in their benefits from those scheduled under current law. For younger workers with average earnings, our proposal involves a gradual reduction in benefits from those scheduled under current law. For example, the reduction in benefits for a 45-year-old average earner is less than 1 percent; for a 35-year-old, less than 5 percent; and for a 25-year-old, less than 9 percent. Reductions are smaller for lower earners, and larger for higher ones.

Our plan combines its gradual benefit reductions with a gradual increase in the payroll tax rate. The combined employer-employee payroll tax rate would rise from 12.4 percent today to 12.5 percent in 2015, 13.2 percent in 2035, 14.2 percent in 2055 and 15.4 percent in 2078; it would continue to rise slowly over time thereafter. This gradual increase in the payroll tax rate slows the decline in replacement rates for any given retirement age.

No Changes in Individual Accounts

Our plan shows that Social Security can be saved without dramatically changing its form. Many recent reform plans have instead replaced part of Social Security with individual accounts. That would be a grave mistake.

Individual accounts, such as 401(k)s and Keoghs, already provide an extremely useful supplement to Social Security, and can be improved and expanded. In our view, however, individual accounts are not a desirable substitute for traditional Social Security, which provides the core layer of financial security during a particular time of need.

This is especially true given the trend in private pensions of moving from defined benefit plans to 401(k)s; that trend increases the correlation between the risks already being borne by workers and the risks that would be borne if individual accounts were to be created.

> *"It is difficult to find any explicit argument favoring PAYGO over funded methods of providing retirement."*

Social Security Should Be Replaced with a Mandatory Private System

Edgar K. Browning

In the following viewpoint, the libertarian economist Edgar K. Browning, a professor at Texas A&M University, attacks the rationale for the current pay-as-you-go (PAYGO) Social Security system. He likens it to deficit spending—it imposes costs on younger people for the benefit of their parents and grandparents. He then illustrates how a mandatory private plan could replace Social Security. Browning's plan would demand much less sacrifice from current workers yet still meet social goals of eliminating poverty among the elderly, providing basic medical insurance, and providing some equity to those who earned less money during their working lives.

Edgar K. Browning, "The Anatomy of Social Security and Medicare," *Independent Review*, vol. XIII, Summer 2008, pp. 19–23. Copyright © 2008 by the Independent Institute. Reproduced by permission of The Independent Institute, 100 Swan Way, Oakland, CA 94021-1428 USA. www.independent.org.

As you read, consider the following questions:

1. According to Browning, what are the three common justifications for the present Social Security system?

2. What evidence does the author offer that most people think the intergenerational transfer of wealth—money from younger people to give to older folks—is immoral?

3. Under Browning's plan, how much would individuals have in savings at the end of a forty-five-year working life?

The three most common justifications given for Social Security are the following. First, many people are too short-sighted to anticipate their retirement needs, and they will not save enough to provide for their own retirement. Second, some people will consciously decide not to save in the expectation that society (that is, government welfare programs) will take care of them in retirement, thereby "gaming the (welfare) system." And third, it is desirable to redistribute income from high-income retirees to low-income retirees.

Why Have Social Security at All?

Let us examine these arguments briefly. The first two can be dealt with together because they simply argue that many people will reach retirement age without sufficient assets to support themselves in retirement. That might be so, although I think it is easy to overstate how many people are likely to be improvident. But do we have to have a government retirement program to take care of these people? There is another option: they can keep working. If someone has not accumulated enough to retire at age sixty-five, is it unreasonable to expect him to work a few more years until he has accumulated enough? Most people are perfectly capable of working into their seventies, and for those who aren't, there are disability benefit programs. It is not clear why the government has to guarantee people a retirement at age sixty-five.

Reservations about the third argument, that Social Security is needed to redistribute income among retired persons, also abound. Redistribution may be desirable, but we do not need Social Security to do it. We might, for example, tax the elderly wealthy to benefit the elderly poor without concealing this operation in Social Security's complicated benefit rules and indeed without having a government retirement program at all. Some defenders of Social Security acknowledge this possibility, but fall back on the contention that the public would not permit as much redistribution if it were done openly. Maybe so, but if the voters will not support this policy openly, is it acceptable to impose it on them in disguise? Many egalitarians answer this question affirmatively; I do not.

Related to the redistribution argument is the contention that one of Social Security's great benefits is that it has reduced poverty among the elderly. It is true that the (official) poverty rate among the elderly has declined . . . with the expansion of Social Security spending: the rate declined from 24.6 percent in 1970 to 10.1 percent in 2005. But that rate would have gone down without Social Security because of the growth in earnings that occurred during this period. Perhaps it would have declined even more without Social Security.

Social Security's Effect on Poverty

In principle, Social Security affects poverty among the elderly in two opposing ways. First, it *increases* poverty by reducing the accumulated assets people bring to retirement (reduced saving), and then it *reduces* poverty by providing the government pension. Which effect is larger is by no means clear. Consider that retirees in the lowest earning categories . . . will receive an implicit rate of return on taxes paid of approximately 3 percent (slightly more for one-earner couples) in 2008. Had they invested these same taxes in a balanced portfolio (60 percent stocks and 40 percent bonds), they would have received a return of approximately 5.5 percent. In view

"Boomers Bummer," by Ed Fischer. www.cartoonstock.com.

of the calculations reported earlier, this difference implies that their retirement income would be more than twice as great had they invested the funds privately. *There would likely be fewer poor among the elderly today if they had been permitted (or required) to save privately when younger rather than participating in Social Security.*

Despite these reservations about the practical significance of the three arguments for Social Security, these arguments do constitute logically valid positions. Yet they provide *no* justification for making a government retirement scheme a PAYGO program, transferring income each year from workers to retirees. As the President's Council of Economic Advisers puts it, "An essential part of this debate [on Social Security] is that none of these rationales require that Social Security be operated on a pay-as-you-go basis." This important point is little understood, as evidenced by the fact that it is difficult to find any explicit argument favoring PAYGO over funded methods of providing retirement.

Can a PAYGO system be defended? To see how one must argue to justify PAYGO financing, recall that the defining characteristic of this policy, the one that distinguishes it from funded alternatives, is that it benefits the early retirees at the expense of later generations. Why should we have a policy that harms all future generations in order to benefit those who retired in the early years of the Social Security system? It is not easy to give a good reason for this type of intergenerational redistribution. . . .

In fact, it is widely accepted that this type of intergenerational redistribution is immoral. One of the major arguments against the use of government deficits is that it unconscionably imposes costs on our children and grandchildren. Yet such an imposition is exactly what PAYGO government retirement programs make. This similarity between deficit finance and PAYGO Social Security is not accidental: when operated on a PAYGO basis, Social Security is just like an elaborate deficit-financed pension program (that's what all the talk about "unfunded liabilities" is about). If deficit finance is unwise or immoral, then so is PAYGO Social Security.

These points, together with the absence of any convincing argument for PAYGO in the mountains of material written on Social Security, are sufficient for us to conclude that no good case can be made for the government's operation of retirement programs on a PAYGO basis.

What Might Have Been

I have asserted that it is not necessary to have a PAYGO system to accommodate the three arguments most commonly made in support of Social Security. I now back up that claim by outlining a policy that satisfies all of these rationales.

Suppose that in 1940 we had begun a retirement program along the following lines (with figures in today's dollars). Each worker is required to contribute 10 percent of the first $12,000 in earnings to a retirement account. These contributions must be invested in a balanced portfolio of stocks and bonds containing 60 percent stocks and 40 percent bonds (chosen from index funds to assure diversification and low administrative costs). At the age of sixty-six (or later if so decided), the individual is required to use the accumulated assets to purchase an annuity, or annual pension, that will continue as long as he lives. The annual benefits will be indexed to inflation to assure no deterioration in purchasing power over the retiree's remaining life.

Note how this plan can satisfy all three of the common arguments for Social Security. Because people are required to save for retirement, no one will reach retirement age without adequate (as we will see) assets to provide a pension. Redistribution can be accommodated (if it is desired) simply by taking some of the assets in some people's accounts (presumably those who are well off) at age sixty-six and adding them to other people's accounts (presumably those who are poor). It is not clear that this redistribution is desirable, but it might be done easily.

Look closer at what we can expect from such a policy. Notice that everyone who earns in excess of $12,000 a year, which is almost everyone who works full time, makes the same contribution of $1,200 a year. That amount will entitle them to (roughly) the same government pension—not exactly the same because people who retire in different years will realize different returns. This pension will not be especially generous, and most people will choose to save privately to supplement it, but it will provide a guaranteed floor of income support for the elderly.

How large a pension will this policy provide? As we have seen, since 1946 this type of investment portfolio has generated a rate of return of 5.5 percent. So if people contributed $1,200 a year for forty-five working years ... at that rate of return the accumulated assets at age sixty-six would be $237,038. That amount can provide an annual pension of $15,407 to every individual worker. That pension exceeds the poverty line for an elderly single person ($9,367 in 2005) and also for an elderly couple ($11,815) by a comfortable margin. So this policy assures that the poverty rate among the elderly will be close to zero.

Additional Benefits

Most elderly people, of course, would not rely solely on this pension. They would save privately to provide additional retirement income, just as many people do today. That saving would yield the higher returns available to private investments rather than the low 1.5 percent return from Social Security. This retirement policy thus effectively creates a floor below which retirement income cannot sink, guaranteeing a minimum amount above the poverty line. Because this result effectively eliminates poverty among the elderly, we may not want or need to redistribute assets among the retired population, but, as stated earlier, such redistribution can easily be made if it is desired.

The returns generated by this policy might also be used to finance health insurance for the elderly. Indeed, the $15,407 pension exceeds the $9,367 poverty line by enough to provide a basic health-insurance policy to the retired person and still leave him with cash income above the poverty line. If we wished to ensure fuller insurance coverage, it would be necessary to increase the contribution rate, say, to 14 percent. That would yield an annual pension of $21,570, nearly $12,000 above the cash poverty line and more than adequate to finance a comprehensive health-insurance policy and provide cash benefits exceeding poverty.

If we had adopted this type of government retirement policy in 1940 instead of PAYGO Social Security, it is probable that all Americans alive today would be better off. There would be no poverty among the retired. Saving and capital accumulation would have been greater, so GDP and wage rates would be greater, and hence low-income (and other) young workers would also be better off. Retirees, of course, would be better off because they would have realized the much higher returns available on private saving.

> "Lifting the payroll tax cap would just about cover the shortfall Social Security will face if economic growth slows to a snail's pace in the decades ahead."

Lifting the Social Security Wage Cap Would Increase Revenues

John Miller

John Miller is a professor of economics at Wheaton College in Illinois and the editor of Real World Banking: A Money and Banking Reader. *In the following viewpoint he advocates eliminating the payroll wage cap on the amount of earnings from employment subject to Social Security taxes. The cap changes yearly with inflation; for example, in 2009 it was $106,000. Wages above that amount are not subject to the 12.4 percent Social Security tax. Miller explains that this means that a small percentage of highly paid workers pay proportionately less in payroll taxes than low and moderately paid employees, making the Social Security tax regressive. He goes on to point out that eliminating the cap would quickly remedy the financial shortfalls the system is heading toward and it's an approach that enjoys wide popular support.*

John Miller, "Go Ahead and Lift the Cap," *Dollars and Sense*, March, 2008. Reproduced by permission of Dollars and Sense, a progressive economics magazine, www.dollars andsense.org.

As you read, consider the following questions:

1. According to the Social Security Administration's Stephen Goss, as cited by Miller, what percentage of the projected Social Security shortfall will be covered by lifting the cap on wages subject to Social Security taxes?

2. What percentage of wages fell under the payroll tax cap in 1983, according to the author?

3. What percentage of wage earners would be affected by lifting the payroll tax cap, according to Miller?

Let's remind ourselves that Social Security, which cut poverty rates among the elderly from 35% in 1960 to 9.4% in 2006, is no Robin Hood plan that robs the rich to pay for the retirement of the working class. Rather, it is a mildly redistributive public retirement program financed by contributions from the wages of working people. In fact, Social Security taxes fall far more heavily on the poor and working class than on the well-to-do. Payroll taxes are a fixed 12.4% (actually 6.2% on employees and 6.2% on employers); they are levied only on wage income, not on property income; and the cap on wages subject to the tax . . . means that while most workers pay the tax on every dollar of their income, the highest earners pay it only on a part.

Even FDR [President Franklin Delano Roosevelt] acknowledged that relying on payroll contributions to finance Social Security was regressive, although he famously argued that with those contributions in place, "no damn politician can ever scrap my Social Security program."

Raising Cap Popular with Voters

[President] George W. Bush's 2005 push to privatize Social Security only underscored FDR's point. Bush made more than 40 trips around the United States to stump for his plan, but fewer people supported Social Security privatization afterwards than before he started. Ironically enough, the only aspect of Social Security reform that has generated widespread support is lifting the cap: in a February 2005 *Washington Post* poll, 81% of respondents agreed that Americans should pay Social Security taxes on wages over the cap.

This is no radical or hare-brained idea. It has the endorsement of the AARP [American Association of Retired Persons], the largest seniors lobby. And there is a clear precedent. A similar cap used to apply to the payroll tax that funds Medicare, but a 1993 law removed that cap and now every dollar of wage income is taxed to pay for Medicare. . . . Lifting the cap would rewrite this one rule to favor working people more. . . .

Lifting the cap on Social Security taxes would raise a significant amount of revenue: $1.3 trillion dollars over ten years according to the libertarian Cato Institute, and $124 billon a year according to the left-of-center Citizens for Tax Justice. Long term, lifting the payroll tax cap would just about cover the shortfall Social Security will face if economic growth slows to a snail's pace in the decades ahead, as forecast by the Social Security Administration (SSA). According to Stephen Goss, the SSA's chief actuary, lifting the cap while giving commensurate benefit hikes to high-income taxpayers once they retire would cover 93% of the SSA's projected shortfall in Social Security revenues over the next 75 years. Removing the cap without raising those benefits would actually produce a surplus in the system over the same period—even if the economy creeps along as the SSA predicts it will.

Finally, the combination of the cap and the unprecedented inequality of the last two decades has shrunk the Social Security tax base. Some 90% of wages fell below the cap in 1983. Today [2008], with the increased concentration of income among the highest-paid, that figure is down to 84%—even as the number of workers with earnings above the cap has dropped. The cap would have to rise to $140,000 just to once again cover 90% of all wages; the additional revenues resulting

Social Security Taxes as a Percentage of Earned Income

$0–10K	11.1%
$10–20K	10.8%
$20–30K	11.0%
$30–40K	11.2%
$40–50K	11.2%
$50–75K	11.3%
$75–100K	11.2%
$100–150K	10.3%
$150–200K	8.5%
$200–300K	6.4%
$300–400K	4.1%
$400–500K	3.3%
$500–750K	2.5%
$750K–1mill	1.9%
$1–2mill	1.2%
$2–5mill	0.6%
$5–10mill	0.3%
$10–20mill	0.1%
$20mill+	0.0%

TAKEN FROM: *Citizens for Tax Justice,* "An Analysis of Eliminating the Cap on Earnings Subject to the Social Security Tax and Related Issues," November 30, 2006. www.ctj.org.

from just this change would close about one-third of the long-term Social Security deficit projected by the SSA.

Hardly Soaking the Rich

Making high earners pay the Social Security tax on all of their wage income, as low- and middle-income earners already have to, might not strike you as class warfare—but the high flyers sure think it is. Just listen to the financial establishment squeal. Investment Management chairman Robert Pozen, architect of the benefit-cutting proposal endorsed by the Bush administration (and deceptively labeled "progressive indexing"), warns that lifting the cap would represent "one of the greatest tax increases of all time" and "is so crazy it's beyond belief." The editors of the *Wall Street Journal* agreed. And the conservative Heritage Foundation ginned up numbers purporting to show that lifting the cap would impose a "massive 12.4 percentage point tax hike" that would return federal tax rates to levels not seen since the 1970s.

Just how wet would the rich get if the cap on Social Security taxes was lifted? The data suggest they would get damp, but hardly soaked.

For starters, lifting the cap affects just 5.9% of wage-earners. This group benefited massively from three rounds of Bush tax cuts, as evidenced by the fact that the effective federal tax rate (i.e., the share of income actually paid in federal taxes, once all deductions and exemptions have been taken) on the richest 5% of taxpayers fell from 31.1% in 2000 to 28.9% in 2005, according to the Congressional Budget Office.

So, lifting the wage cap on Social Security taxes would not do much more than reverse those tax giveaways to the wealthy. And the wealthiest taxpayers, those with incomes over $1 million, would still be paying a smaller portion of their income in payroll taxes than all other taxpayers. For the top 5% of taxpayers, lifting the cap would push their effective federal tax rate up to 31.5%, a bit above where it was when Bush took office but still below the 31.8% level they paid back in 1979, before nearly three decades of pro-rich tax cutting. The top 1% would pay an effective federal tax rate of 33.8%—again, higher than it was in 2000 but still well below its 1979 level of 37.0%.

That is hardly soaking the rich. In any case they can afford it. The best-off 5% of households had an average income of $520,200 in 2005, some 81% higher than in 1979 after correcting for inflation. The richest 1%, with an average income of $1,558,500 in 2005, saw their after-tax income rise a whopping 176% over the same period.

Lifting the cap on payroll taxes would not only resolve any alleged crisis in Social Security, but also help to right the economic wrongs of the last few decades. And it is popular to boot. Isn't that an idea any progressive politician should seriously consider?

> "Raising the Social Security wage cap would be damaging and does not reform the program."

Lifting the Social Security Wage Cap Will Not Save the System

David C. John and Rea S. Hederman Jr.

Income above a certain level is not subject to payroll contributions to Social Security. This may seem unfair, but in the viewpoint that follows two Heritage Foundation scholars argue for leaving this cap in place. They contend that the cap benefits mostly well-off but not wealthy workers and that it also helps those who are nearing retirement. Moreover, the authors predict small businesses would also end up paying more tax if the cap were lifted creating negative effects in the economy.

David C. John is a scholar specializing in economic policy at the Heritage Foundation, where Rea S. Hederman Jr. is a senior data analyst.

As you read, consider the following questions:

1. According to the authors, what percentage of taxpayers would be affected by eliminating the maximum income (the "cap") subject to Social Security taxes?

2. How many job opportunities do John and Hederman estimate will be lost if the cap is lifted?

3. What are some examples given by the authors of professions that would pay more tax if the cap was lifted?

Raising someone else's taxes may seem like a painless solution when a government program starts running deficits. For instance, in 2017 Social Security will begin to spend more in benefits than it takes in from payroll taxes, and some interest groups believe that the ideal solution is to simply increase taxes on "wealthier" Americans.

Raising payroll taxes is the wrong solution to Social Security's long term financing problem, and it is not the way to achieve retirement security for Americans. The wiser approach is to view Social Security reform in the context of comprehensive retirement income reform. That means taking steps to strengthen retirement savings as well as Social Security and reviewing the tax treatment of retirement programs and savings plans as well as the structure of Social Security benefits.

The Wage Cap

A cap on taxable earnings has existed since the inception of the Social Security system in 1937. Currently, workers pay Social Security payroll taxes on only the first $97,500 of their annual income (as of January 1, 2007; in 2006, workers paid Social Security taxes on their first $94,200 in wages). This "wage cap" is indexed to the growth of real wages in the economy and increases every year. The wage cap serves to limit the amount of Social Security benefits that a well-off retiree will receive. Even though Bill Gates and Donald Trump earn millions of dollars a year, for the purpose of calculating Social Security benefits, they earned just $97,500 in 2007.

The Economic Impact

Raising the amount of earnings subject to Social Security payroll taxes would do nothing to address the wider challenge of securing retirement for working Americans. Moreover, it would have real and damaging effects on working families and the U.S. economy. Some would dismiss the negative effects by noting that "only" about 6.5 percent of taxpayers would be affected, but a large proportion of those whose taxes would increase earn less than $125,000 annually. While these workers are not poor, neither are they wealthy. Subjecting all earnings to Social Security payroll taxes would:

- Reduce the annual take-home pay of 10.3 million workers by an average of $5,650 in the first year alone after the cap is removed. Most of these workers have incomes below $125,000.

- Raise taxes on 4.0 million workers over the age of 50—just when they are trying to steer towards retirement.

- Raise taxes on 3 million small business owners.

- Greatly increase the top effective federal marginal tax rate.

- Weaken the U.S. economy by reducing the number of job opportunities and workers' personal savings. By fiscal year 2015, the number of job opportunities lost would exceed 965,000, and personal savings would decline by more than $55 billion, in real terms.

- Not save Social Security. A 2003 Social Security Administration study showed that eliminating the Social Security wage cap would delay the program's deficits for only about six years.

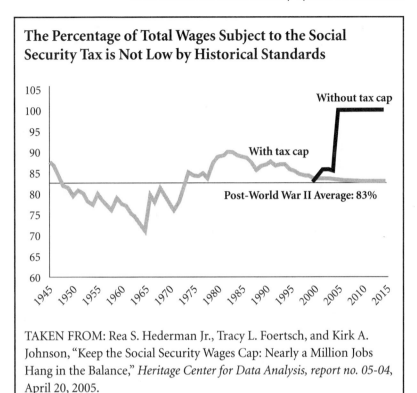

The Percentage of Total Wages Subject to the Social Security Tax is Not Low by Historical Standards

TAKEN FROM: Rea S. Hederman Jr., Tracy L. Foertsch, and Kirk A. Johnson, "Keep the Social Security Wages Cap: Nearly a Million Jobs Hang in the Balance," *Heritage Center for Data Analysis, report no. 05-04,* April 20, 2005.

Rather than focus on raising the wage cap, Congress should develop a comprehensive solution to Social Security's future deficits that examines all aspects of the program and places a strong emphasis on increasing personal savings across all income levels. This approach would be the first step towards placing all entitlement programs on a sound financial footing and protecting our children and grandchildren from having to deal with those program's massive deficits.

Stifling Marginal Tax Rates

If Social Security's wage cap were raised, many workers would immediately find that federal taxes consume over 43 cents of every additional dollar that they earn. While raising the wage cap is sold with the rhetorical point that "Those who have benefited from the growth in the economy should be asked to pay a little more to help secure Social Security," the fact is that it would mostly hurt the middle class.

By raising the wage cap to $140,000, a single worker earning $110,000 would see his or her marginal tax rate increase from approximately 31 percent to 43 percent, plus any state or local income tax. A married couple in which the sole-earner makes $110,000 will see their marginal tax rate increase from 28 percent to 40 percent. If the other spouse also works and makes $40,000, the couple would face a marginal tax rate of 43 percent for both earners. For the highest income workers, the marginal tax rate would rise from 38.4 percent to about 53 percent—a level not seen since the 1970s.

An October 2003 report from the Social Security Administration (SSA) examined the effects of not just raising the wage cap, but of eliminating it completely. Under this radical approach, Bill Gates and Donald Trump would pay Social Security taxes on every dollar that they earn. They would also receive benefits on those earnings. The SSA study showed that eliminating the payroll tax cap entirely would only delay the start of Social Security's annual deficits by six years. If completely eliminating the wage cap only delays Social Security's coming deficits by six years, just raising it would not solve a significant part of Social Security's financial problems.

Who Would Pay More?

Raising the wage cap does not mainly affect the rich. For every taxpayer with an income of over $500,000 affected by raising the tax cap to $125,000, 24 taxpayers with lower incomes would pay higher taxes. In 2004, the majority of taxpayers earning more than $90,000 had incomes between $90,000 and $150,000. Only a very small number of the 132 million tax returns filed in 2004 (0.33 percent of taxpayers) showed income between $500,000 and $1 million, and an even smaller number (0.18 percent) showed incomes over $1 million.

In addition, raising the wage cap does not target just executives or the wealthy. Increasing the wage cap above $97,500 would raise the taxes of 71,214 elementary and middle school teachers, 97,065 carpenters, 110,908 policemen and policewomen, 254,992 nurses, 208,562 post-secondary teachers, and 237,000 dentists.

Voters Want Social Security Fixed

A December 2006 poll showed that Americans want Congress to fix Social Security. The Rasmussen survey of 1000 likely voters showed that 57 percent felt that Social Security needed to be fixed, while only 30 percent wanted the program to be left alone. Other polls show that Americans want Congress to work on a bipartisan basis to address key issues such as entitlement reform.

Fixing Social Security will require bold leadership. Raising the Social Security wage cap would be damaging and does not reform the program. Some steps have to be considered to rein in the costs of the program, such as raising the retirement age, instituting lower promised benefits for younger workers, and modifying the cost-of-living adjustment formulas. But a comprehensive approach to fixing Social Security also requires a comprehensive overhaul of America's system of retirement financing, including personal savings and the tax treatment of retirement plans and programs.

Congress should not try to take the "easy" approach to dealing with Social Security. While raising Social Security's wage cap would provide more money to the program and delay the coming annual deficits for a few years, it would also hurt the economy and the millions of workers with incomes just above the wage cap. In addition, after such a tax increase, our children would still be left with a Social Security program that has promised more in benefits than it can afford to pay.

Instead, Congress should consider a comprehensive approach that recognizes America's changing demographics and creates a sustainable Social Security system that can afford to pay adequate benefits to those who need them the most. Most importantly, a comprehensive solution to Social Security should also enable workers of all income levels to build personal savings, part of which they could use to enhance their Social Security benefits or to leave a nest egg to their children. Such a reform would enable Social Security to provide workers with the same kind of retirement security that our parents and grandparents achieved.

> *"Simplifying Social Security benefits should be a priority when reform is addressed."*

Simplifying Social Security Should Be a Priority of Reform Efforts

Andrew G. Biggs

Andrew G. Biggs, currently a resident scholar at the American Enterprise Institute, is a former principal deputy commissioner of the Social Security Administration. In the viewpoint that follows, he makes the case that Social Security's complex formula for computing benefits subjects Americans to financial risk. Because a substantial number of workers significantly overestimate the amount they will receive from the government pension program, they could be short of funds when it is time to retire, Biggs contends. Making the system simpler would help Americans to better predict what their benefits will be, he maintains.

As you read, consider the following questions:

1. According to the author, why is it detrimental to *underestimate* future Social Security benefits?

Andrew G. Biggs, "Answer Quickly: How Much Do You Think You'll Get from Social Security," *AEI Online*, June 19, 2009. Copyright © 2009 American Enterprise Institute for Public Policy Research. Reproduced with the permission of the American Enterprise Institute for Public Policy Research, Washington, D.C.

2. When Americans were asked about how much Social Security they would receive, by how much did one-quarter of the respondents overestimate their projected benefits, according to Biggs?

3. What two nations does the author say have "flatter"— and thus easier to predict, pension benefits systems?

This year [2009], one in four new retirees will discover that their largest retirement income source falls 28 percent or more below their expectations. But that asset is not a recession-battered 401(k) account. It is Social Security. To understand why, answer quickly: how much do you think your Social Security benefit will be? If you do not know, you are in good company. Due to the complexity of Social Security's benefit formula, a worryingly large proportion of Americans have no idea what their Social Security benefit will be until the first check arrives. This "predictability risk" is just as costly as the market risk associated with 401(k) plans. Simplifying Social Security benefits should be a priority when reform is addressed.

A principal advantage of a traditional defined-benefit pension plan over defined-contribution plans like individual retirement accounts and 401(k)s is the predictability of future retirement benefits. The Federal Citizen Information Center calls defined-benefit pensions "a predictable, secure pension for life," saying that "workers are promised a specific benefit at retirement . . . [and] can know in advance what benefits they will receive."

Unlike defined-contribution plans, in which plan participants bear the risk of fluctuating stock and bond values, defined-benefit plans pay a set benefit that individuals should be able to predict well in advance. Knowing with precision what their retirement benefits will be allows individuals to make better decisions regarding how much to save on their own and when to leave the workforce.

Social Security provides a defined benefit. In debates over how to restore Social Security's solvency and whether to incorporate personal retirement accounts into the program, Social Security's "predictable, stable retirement income," in AARP's [American Association of Retired Persons] words, has been touted as a reason to retain its traditional benefit structure without reductions or diversification into personal accounts.

This position is undercut, however, if individuals are not able to predict their future benefits accurately. A defined benefit that is difficult to predict due to the complexity of its benefit formula carries "predictability risk" in the same way that a defined-contribution retirement carries market risk. In both cases, individuals may find themselves with retirement incomes that differ significantly from what they anticipated. Those who overestimate their retirement incomes are at greatest risk. However, even those who underestimate their future benefits pay a price because of oversaving during their working years. This excess saving sacrifices other opportunities, such as pursuing further education, purchasing a home, or starting a business.

A predictable Social Security benefit helps working-age individuals decide how much to save on their own to create an adequate retirement income. Unpredictability means that too many individuals discover their error after it is too late to do much about it.

The Benefit Formula

What makes Social Security benefits so hard to predict? First, consider how a typical private-sector, defined-benefit pension is calculated: workers simply multiply a percentage of their final salary by the number of years of employment. This allows for relatively easy estimates of future retirement benefits that can be updated on the fly.

But for Social Security, benefits are calculated by indexing a worker's past earnings to the growth of average national wages. This involves multiplying the ratio of earnings in a past year to average wages economy-wide in that year by the average wage in the year the worker turned sixty. Earnings past age sixty are not indexed. Next, Social Security averages the highest thirty-five years of indexed earnings. These average earnings are then run through a progressive benefit formula to produce the Primary Insurance Amount payable at the full retirement age, currently sixty-six. For a new retiree in 2009, Social Security replaces 90 percent of the first $744 in average monthly earnings, 32 percent of earnings between $745 and $4,483, and 15 percent of earnings above $4,483. These dollar amounts increase each year along with average wage growth in the economy.

However, if this benefit is less than half of the benefit received by the higher-earning spouse in a married couple, the lower-earning spouse is eligible to receive a spousal benefit instead. Spousal benefits may be collected off the earnings record of a former spouse—but only if the marriage lasted at least ten years.

Whatever benefit is received is then reduced or increased based on whether benefits are claimed before or after the full retirement age, which is itself increasing for those born between 1954 and 1959. Finally, the retirement earnings test may reduce benefits for early claimants who continue working. Few Americans are aware, however, that at the full retirement age, benefits are increased to account for reductions due to the earnings test. To say the least, these are not back-of-the-envelope calculations.

Many Overestimate Benefits

How bad is the problem? The Health and Retirement Study (HRS), a federally funded survey of older Americans, allows us to compare near-retirees' predictions of their future Social

"I fondly remember the time before the money ran out."

"I fondly remember the time before the money ran out," by Andrew Toos. www.cartoonstock.com.

Security benefits to what those benefits actually turned out to be. My analysis builds upon similar studies by [Social Security Administration economists] Alan L. Gustman and Thomas L. Steinmeier and Susann Rohwedder and Arthur van Soest. I use data from the 2000, 2002, 2004, and 2006 waves of the HRS. In these years, individuals were asked at what age they expected to start collecting benefits, followed by: "If you start collecting Social Security benefits then, about how much do you expect the payments to be in today's dollars?" Individuals who have already claimed benefits are asked what their Social Security benefit is. . . .

Almost one in four individuals on the verge of retirement could or would not even hazard a guess as to their Social Security benefit level. Of those who could make a prediction, guesses were close to accurate on average—but only on average. While the median prediction underestimated realized benefits by only 3 percent, one-third of near-retirees overestimated their benefits by at least 10 percent, while one-quarter overestimated them by more than 28 percent. One in ten retirees was to receive a benefit of less than half as much as he expected.

Similar numbers underestimate their future benefits. This is important, as it implies that a single uniform error—such as a failure to account for the effects of inflation on future benefits—is not responsible for the misestimates of benefits observed in HRS data. . . .

Put simply, a significant number of Americans have no idea what their "predictable, reliable" Social Security benefit will be until the first check arrives. It is difficult to see how this "predictability risk" differs in substance from the market risk inherent in defined-contribution retirement accounts. In both cases, there is the chance that the income derived from the retirement vehicle may differ from the level expected prior to retirement. In the case of defined-contribution accounts, however, the individual has the option to reduce that risk by investing in more stable, but lower-returning, assets. Under Social Security's benefit formula, however, predictability risk is difficult to eliminate. The only thing an individual can do is take steps to inform himself as retirement approaches. . . .

Potential Reforms

One wholesale reform to improve the understandability and predictability of benefits is a flat dollar payment to each retiree—some call this a "citizens' pension"—supplemented by individual savings in a personal account. For instance, New Zealand's universal pension plan pays a benefit equal to 42 percent of per-capita gross domestic product, supplemented by the more recent KiwiSaver accounts. Likewise, the United

Kingdom is shifting toward a flatter defined benefit, adjusted for years of labor force participation, supplemented by individual savings accounts. In either case, the uniformity of the base benefit would cause its value to be well-known and better understood, making other saving decisions easier. Combined with individual saving, a flat dollar benefit could provide the same level of benefits and progressivity as current-law Social Security but in a significantly simpler package.

Many options are available, but the key is for policymakers to accept the difficulty many Americans have in understanding how their Social Security benefits are calculated. While the temptations to fine-tune the benefit formula are many, the predictability risk they create imposes significant costs on American retirees. While improved notification of Social Security benefits is important, this alone will not fully address the problem.

Periodical Bibliography

The following articles have been selected to supplement the diverse views presented in this chapter.

Aaron Bernstein, Howard Gleckman, and Michael J. Mandel
"Social Security: Three New Ideas," *Business-Week*, February 21, 2005.

Jason Burrell
"Counterpoint: The Case Against Social Security Reform," *International Social Science Review*, January 2005.

Patrick Dattalo
"Borrowing to Save: A Critique of Recent Proposals to Partially Privatize Social Security," *Social Work*, July 2007.

Gerald P. Dwyer Jr.
"Social Security Private Accounts: A Risky Proposition?" *Economic Review*, no. 3, 2005.

Michael Finke and Swarnankur Chatterjee
"Social Security: Who Wants Private Accounts?" *Financial Services Review*, Winter 2008.

Thomas A. Garrett and Russell M. Rhine
"Social Security Versus Private Retirement Accounts: A Historical Analysis," *Federal Reserve Bank of Saint Louis Review*, March/April 2005. www.research.stlouisfed.org.

Michael Hudson
"The $4.7 Trillion Pyramid," *Harper's*, April 2005.

Barbara B. Kennelly
"Myths and Realities About Social Security and Privatization," *Generations*, Spring 2005.

Roger Lowenstein
"A Question of Numbers," *New York Times Magazine*, January 16, 2005.

David Moberg
"'Ownership' Swindle," *Nation*, April 4, 2005.

John O'Neil
"Risky Business," *NEA Today*, April 2005.

Ramesh Ponnuru
"An Idea Whose Time Has Come," *National Review*, January 31, 2005.

OPPOSING
VIEWPOINTS®
SERIES

CHAPTER 3

How Does Social Security Affect Different Social Groups?

Chapter Preface

A ny change in a program like Social Security will have different implications for different social groups. Depending on which reforms are adopted, African Americans, women, people with disabilities, and other groups might see average payments that go to members of their group increase or decrease. For this reason advocates for these groups watch debates over Social Security carefully. By the same token, promoters of various reform plans seek to appeal to specific communities, claiming their plan will benefit the group being targeted.

The debate over women's stake in Social Security and its reform is a good example of how advocates of rival reform plans seek the support of particular groups. Due to women's employment patterns and longer life expectancy, women are more likely than men to become reliant on Social Security. Aware of this, both proponents and opponents of privatization have tailored their message to appeal to the nation's female population. Those favoring privatization claim that individual accounts will help women, who often interrupt their careers for childcare or other reasons, accumulate retirement savings. Opponents claim that a privatized Social Security system will put women at risk.

Social Security benefits paid out at retirement are dependent on lifetime earnings. Despite changes in gender roles in the last few decades, women are still more likely than men to take time out from a career to raise children. Periods of stay-at-home child care, during which the woman does not earn wages, bring down her Social Security benefits relative to her spouse. Privatization proponents have suggested that mandatory individual retirement accounts could solve this problem. Individuals would be required to invest a certain amount of income in a retirement account. In the case of married couples, the sole earner would be required to invest an equal amount in his or her partner's account. By law, a husband would be required to deposit the same amount of money into his wife's account as he deposited to his own. The law would, of course, apply to the less common case of working wives with stay-at-home husbands. Because such accounts are separate, each partner would be protected in case the marriage broke up. Each would simply keep what had accumulated in their own account, regardless if the money came originally from their own wages or from their spouse's. In a 1998 analysis for the free-market-oriented Cato Institute, researchers Ekaterina Shirley and Peter Spiegler concluded that mandatory individual retirement accounts would benefit women. "Under a properly designed system of individually owned, privately invested accounts, with a provision for earnings sharing between spouses, women would likely be significantly better off than under the current system," they concluded.

Opponents of privatization say that contrary to the analyses of privatization advocates, women benefit disproportionately from the current Social Security system. While higher earners do receive more benefits, lower earners receive disproportionately high benefits relative to lifetime earnings. Because they earn less on average, having lower wage earners receive more benefits in proportion to former income benefits women. Moreover, Social Security currently has provisions for crediting spouses with income earned by their partners if the couple splits; this eliminates some of the advantage individual accounts have in the event of divorce; however, opponents say that the key reason privatization is a bad policy for women is that women's smaller incomes disadvantage them in the investment market. "Because low earners have less money to invest and cannot afford risky investments, it is likely that they will have lower rates of return on their individual accounts," opine Catherine Hill and Caroline Wall of the Institute for Women's Policy Research.

Other groups face similar considerations of how their members will be affected by Social Security reform. The authors in the following chapter explore how changes in the system could affect women, African Americans, and people with disabilities.

"One in three disabled workers and nearly two out of three [Supplemental Security Income] recipients suffer from a mental disorder; respectively, double and triple the proportions since the 1970s."

The Mentally Ill Are Straining Social Security Disability Programs

Jennifer L. Erkulwater

Jennifer L. Erkulwater is a professor of political science at the University of Richmond in Virginia.

In the following viewpoint, Erkulwater shows that Disability Insurance (DI) and Supplemental Security Income (SSI) are important sources of aid to the disabled. The first program is aimed at disabled former workers, while the second helps those who may never have had a job. The number of people receiving money from both programs is increasing, Erkulwater argues, driven by awards to the mentally disabled. Erkulwater contends that be-

Jennifer L. Erkulwater, *Disability Rights and the American Social Safety Net*. Ithaca, NY: Cornell University Press, 2006, pp. 5–24. Copyright © 2006 by Cornell University. Used by permission of the publisher, Cornell University Press.

cause mental illnesses are often vaguely defined and not readily apparent, the situation has led to administrative and political trouble for these programs.

As you read, consider the following questions:

1. How much money was spent on disabled benefits in 2003, according to Erkulwater?

2. What examples of "soft" impairments are cited by the author?

3. What does Erkulwater cite critics as saying about eligibility standards for disability benefits today compared to the 1950s?

Social Security actually includes two programs for the disabled: Disability Insurance (DI) and Supplemental Security Income (SSI). The two programs share the same definition of disability and rules for certification. The difference is that DI is a social insurance program that provides benefits only to workers who have paid into the program's trust fund and to the dependents of those workers. SSI, on the other hand, is a source of cash support for individuals who live in poverty. In addition, how much a worker and his family receive from DI depends on the amount the worker contributed in payroll taxes, while SSI benefits, meager by comparison, are designed only to bring the recipient's income close to the poverty line. By any measure used, DI has expanded significantly since 1956 when Congress agreed to insure workers against the economic risks of disablement. SSI, added in 1972, has also grown by leaps and bounds. The number of persons awarded DI and SSI was especially pronounced in the years 1972–75 and 1984–95. A commensurate increase in program costs matched this expansion in program participation. Total federal and state spending for SSI increased from $3.8 billion in 1974 to $35 billion in 2003, with particularly rapid growth taking place during the 1990s. Meanwhile, total spending for DI benefits tripled from $3.2 billion in 1970 to $10.4 billion in 1976. By 1986, costs had nearly doubled to $20.5 billion; they then more than doubled again to $42.0 billion in 1996. In 2003, spending on benefits for disabled workers and their families reached $66 billion.

Difficult to Verify

More important than sheer enrollment numbers and expenditure levels, however, were three trends that accompanied growth. First was the fact that this expansion in spending and enrollment did not occur evenly among groups of the disabled. Instead, it was concentrated among impairments that are difficult to measure and verify—impairments such as chronic pain, backaches, fatigue, muscle weakness, and anxiety. Mental disorders are the most common of these "soft" impairments. . . . Presently, one in three disabled workers and nearly two out of three SSI recipients suffer from a mental disorder; respectively, these are double and triple the proportions since the 1970s. The prevalence of mental disabilities is even more striking among children enrolled in SSI. Between 1989 and 2001, the proportion of children with a mental impairment grew more than fivefold, increasing from only 6 percent of all children receiving SSI to 32 percent. Today, children and adults with mental disorders outnumber beneficiaries in all other diagnostic categories.

More Mentally Ill

The rising numbers of beneficiaries with mental disorders contributed to a second trend that accompanied the expansion of DI and SSI—that is, the growing presence of younger people on the disability rolls. Because some of the most severe mental illnesses occur in young adulthood and can disrupt education plans and budding careers in a way that will have a lasting impact on future employment prospects, beneficiaries with mental impairments are, on the whole, younger than

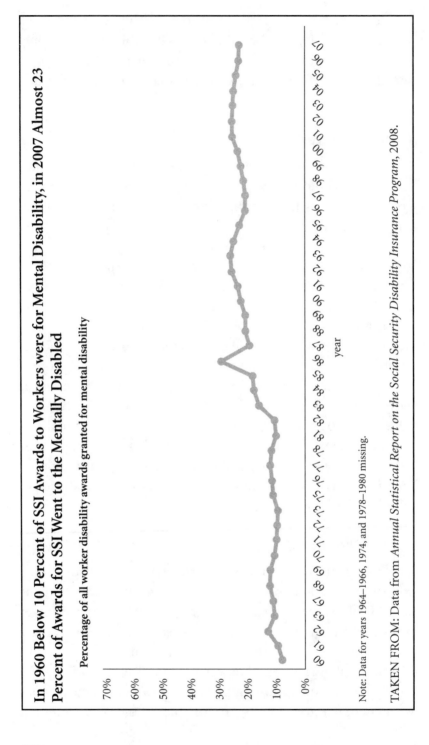

In 1960 Below 10 Percent of SSI Awards to Workers were for Mental Disability, in 2007 Almost 23 Percent of Awards for SSI Went to the Mentally Disabled

Percentage of all worker disability awards granted for mental disability

Note: Data for years 1964–1966, 1974, and 1978–1980 missing.

TAKEN FROM: Data from *Annual Statistical Report on the Social Security Disability Insurance Program*, 2008.

beneficiaries with other conditions. Thus, as mental disorders became more prominent on the disability rolls, the age of the typical person receiving disability payments dropped precipitously. Between 1960 and 1993, the average age of workers enrolled in DI fell from 54.5 years to an all-time low of 47.7 years. (It has since rebounded to 51.3 years). Because SSI pays benefits to children, its recipients, on average, tend to be even younger than DI beneficiaries. Currently, one-third of SSI recipients are under the age of 40 compared to only 14 percent of disabled workers. But even when children are excluded from the calculations, almost twice as many adult SSI recipients as disabled workers are under the age of 40, largely because SSI enrolls a larger proportion of people with mental impairments than DI does and because DI claimants must show a history of employment before they qualify while SSI applicants do not.

The larger proportion of mental disorders and the relative youth of current DI and SSI beneficiaries contributed to a third trend associated with program expansion. Given that persons with mental disorders tend to stay on the disability rolls longer than anyone else, as the average age of beneficiaries dropped, the length of time that the typical beneficiary received disability payments increased. According to [researchers] Kalman Rupp and Charles Scott, a disabled worker entering Disability Insurance today is expected to collect benefits for an average of 10.9 years, up from an expected duration of 9.5 years in 1975. SSI recipients are expected to stay on the rolls even longer. Rupp and Scott estimate that the adults and children presently enrolled in SSI will, on average, spend the next 17.8 years receiving payments.

Political and Administrative Trouble

Taken together, these three trends—the growing prevalence of mental disorders and other soft impairments, the increasing youth of beneficiaries, and longer spells on the disability rolls—add up to administrative and political trouble. In recent decades, the Social Security Administration (SSA) has struggled to find a reliable way of evaluating mental disorders, one that will adequately separate true medical conditions from mere personality flaws. Critics, meanwhile, remain dissatisfied, arguing that people who are found disabled today simply do not meet the strict standard of disability that Congress intended when it created DI in the 1950s. At the same time, given the relative youth of DI and SSI beneficiaries, some lawmakers have urged the SSA to intensify its rehabilitation and employment support efforts rather than simply send out disability checks. Indeed, some elected officials now worry that the long stretches that DI beneficiaries and especially SSI recipients spend collecting payments will not only encourage long-term "welfare" dependency among the disabled, a term once reserved for single mothers, but also push program costs higher far into the future.

*"Four of the five [Social Security] re-
form elements that we analyzed would
reduce total lifetime benefits for more
than three-quarters of disabled workers
and dependents."*

Proposed Reforms Will
Reduce Social Security
Payments to the Disabled

Barbara D. Bovbjerg

*The U.S. Government Accountability Office (GAO), known as
"the congressional watchdog," supports Congress in meeting its
constitutional responsibilities and helps improve the performance
and accountability of the federal government.*

*In the following viewpoint, the GAO presents the results of
simulations that project how disability benefits would be affected
by various Social Security reform proposals—what it terms "reform elements." The simulations showed that most reforms would
reduce benefits to the disabled, though some would have more
impact than others.*

As you read, consider the following questions:

1. What changes have been suggested to improve solvency
   of the Social Security system, according to the author?

Barbara D. Bovbjerg, "Social Security Reform: Issues for Disability and Dependent Benefits," *GAO Reports*, November 26, 2007, pp. 12–15, 17, 19–20.

2. Which reform would have the largest impact on disabled workers and dependents, in the GAO's view?

3. Which suggested change would have the least impact on disabled workers and dependents, according to the author?

Social Security is currently financed primarily on a pay-as-you-go basis, in which payroll tax contributions of current workers are used primarily to pay for current benefits. Since the mid-1980s, the Social Security program has collected more in taxes than it has paid out in benefits. However, because of the retirement of the baby boomers coupled with increases in life expectancy, and decreases in the fertility rate, this situation will soon reverse itself. According to the Social Security Administration's 2007 intermediate assumptions, annual cash surpluses are predicted to turn into ever-growing cash deficits beginning in 2017. Absent changes to the program, these deficits are projected to deplete the Social Security DI [Disability Insurance] trust fund in 2026 and the OASI [Old-Age and Survivors Insurance] trust fund in 2042, leaving the combined system unable to pay full benefits by 2041. Reductions in benefits, increases in revenues, or a combination of both will likely be needed to restore long-term solvency. A number of proposals have been made to restore fiscal solvency to the program, and many include revenue enhancements, benefit reductions, or structural changes such as the introduction of individual accounts as a part of Social Security. Because many reforms to the benefit side of the equation would reduce benefits through changes in the benefit formula, they could affect DI and dependents' benefits as well as Old Age benefits. Unless accompanied by offsets or protections, these reforms might reduce the income of disabled workers and dependents. This situation could be challenging for these beneficiaries as they may have relatively low incomes or higher health care costs and rely heavily on Social Security income. Many disabled workers and dependents may also have trouble taking on additional work and accumulating more savings and, thus, have difficulty preparing for Social Security benefit reductions.

Many reform elements could have a substantial impact on the benefits of Social Security recipients, including those of disabled workers and dependents. We considered six such elements that have been included in reform proposals to improve trust fund solvency. These reform elements take a variety of forms and would change either the initial benefit calculation or the growth of individual benefits over time. Our projections indicated that most of these elements would reduce benefits from currently scheduled levels for the majority of both disabled workers and dependents. That is, most would reduce median lifetime benefits for these beneficiary types—some more substantially than others. Many of these beneficiaries would also experience a reduction in total lifetime benefits; the extent of which would depend on the reform element and individual.

Reform Proposals

We considered six different reform elements that could help control costs and improve Social Security solvency by reducing benefits. Five would change how initial benefits are calculated, and one would limit the growth of an individual's benefits over time.

We considered several ways to improve solvency:

- Longevity indexing would lower the amount of the initial benefit in order to reflect projected increases in life expectancy. Such indexing would maintain relatively comparable levels of lifetime benefits across birth years by proportionally reducing the replacement factors in the initial benefit formula.

- Price indexing would maintain purchasing power while slowing the growth of initial benefits. This would be accomplished by indexing initial benefits to the growth in prices rather than wages, as wages tend to increase faster than prices.

- Progressive price indexing, a form of price indexing, would control costs while protecting the benefits of those beneficiaries at the lowest earnings levels (in terms of career average earnings). It would continue to index initial benefit levels to wages for those below a certain earnings threshold and employ a graduated combination of price indexing and wage indexing for those above this threshold.

- Increasing the number of years used in the benefit calculation would also control program costs. For example, initial benefits could be based on the highest 40, rather than 35, years of indexed earnings. This could be done either by eliminating the 5 years normally excluded from the calculation or by increasing the total number of years factored in from 40 to 45 years. In either of these cases, the initial Old Age benefit would be calculated using the highest 40 years of indexed earnings.

- Raising the age at which people are eligible for full retirement benefits could change the amount and/or the timing of initial benefits. Increasing the full retirement age would improve solvency by generally increasing the number of years worked, reducing the number of years benefits are received and increasing revenue to the system through payroll taxes in the additional years worked. Further, those who retire early would have their benefits actuarially [according to insurance statistics] reduced.

- Though it would not generally affect initial benefit amounts, a change to Social Security's cost-of-living adjustment (COLA) could also control costs and im-

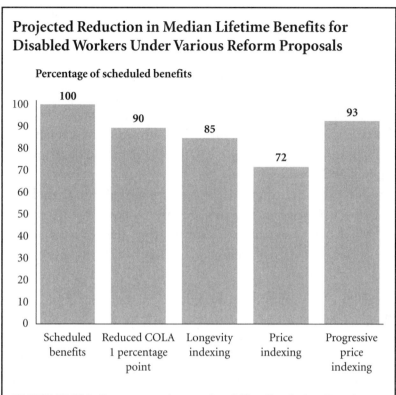

Projected Reduction in Median Lifetime Benefits for Disabled Workers Under Various Reform Proposals

Percentage of scheduled benefits

TAKEN FROM: Government Accounting Office Simulation Data in Barbara D. Bovbjerg, "Social Security Reform: Issues for Disability and Dependent Benefits," *GAO Reports*, November 26, 2007.

prove solvency by limiting the growth of an individual's benefits over time. The COLA adjusts benefits to account for inflation by indexing benefits to price growth annually, using the Consumer Price Index (CPI). Setting the COLA below the CPI would limit the nominal growth of an individual's benefits over time, and as such those who receive benefits for a prolonged period of time would see the largest reductions.

Most Proposals Reduce Benefits

According to our projections for the 1985 cohort [i.e., those born that year], four of the five reform elements that we analyzed would reduce total lifetime benefits for more than three-quarters of disabled workers and dependents, relative to currently scheduled benefits. . . . For three of the elements—reducing the COLA by one percentage point, price indexing and progressive price indexing—the percentage of disabled workers affected is very similar to the percentage of dependents affected. Moreover, for these three reform elements, more than 99 percent, or virtually all, disabled workers and dependents would see their benefits reduced. In contrast, progressive price indexing differs from other reform elements in its impact: fewer beneficiaries are affected, and the percentage of disabled workers affected varies from that of dependents. While an estimated 87 percent of dependents would experience a reduction in lifetime benefits under progressive price indexing, an estimated 77 percent of disabled workers would do so.

While the COLA reduction, longevity indexing and price indexing are all designed in such a way that they affect virtually all beneficiaries, the COLA, which has a greater impact on solvency than longevity indexing, affects relatively fewer disabled workers and dependents. This is because the COLA reduction would first affect benefits one year after the initial benefit payment was made, whereas both longevity indexing and price indexing affect the initial benefit amount. Our simulations indicated that 1.11 percent of disabled workers died within the first year of receiving benefits, while only 0.35 percent of dependents did so. Most such beneficiaries would not have received a COLA.

According to our simulations each of the reform elements we selected would reduce median lifetime benefits for both disabled workers and dependents relative to currently scheduled benefits. However, our projections also indicated that these reductions would vary by reform element. Price indexing would have the largest impact on disabled workers and dependents, reducing median lifetime benefits by more than

25 percent. Median lifetime benefits would fall from $473,960 to $343,350 for disabled workers and from $351,910 to $244,745 for dependents. Progressive price indexing, on the other hand, would create the smallest reduction in median lifetime benefits, with median lifetime benefits falling by 7 percent for disabled workers and 8 percent for dependents.

> "A black man or woman ... paying ex-
> actly the same lifetime Social Security
> taxes as his or her white counterpart,
> will likely receive far less in lifetime
> Social Security benefits."

Privatizing Social Security Will Help African Americans

Michael Tanner

*Michael Tanner is a senior fellow at the libertarian Cato Insti-
tute. His research focuses on welfare and retirement policy.*

*Tanner makes the case in the following viewpoint that the
current Social Security system hinders savings and wealth for-
mation among poorer groups, including—on average—African
Americans. Currently Social Security prevents the poor from
building up private wealth that can be passed along to heirs,
Tanner contends, contributing to a wealth gap between blacks
and whites. Moreover, he contends, because blacks as a group do
not live as long as whites, they do not receive the same amount
of Social Security benefits. Tanner believes that personal social
security accounts that are owned by each worker would alleviate
these problems and provide all beneficiaries with inheritable
wealth.*

Michael Tanner, "Testimony Before the Subcommittee on Social Security," United States
House of Representatives, Committee on Ways and Means, May 25, 2005. Reproduced
by permission of the author.

As you read, consider the following questions:

1. What percentage of retirement income do the richest 20 percent of Americans receive from Social Security, according to Tanner?

2. According to the author, what proportion of African Americans over the age of sixty-five are below the poverty level?

3. Are workers who die soon after retirement able to pass the money they contributed to the Social Security system on to their heirs, in Tanner's opinion?

It is now generally acknowledged that Social Security is facing severe future financing problems: The program will begin running deficits in just 12 years, and is facing total unfunded obligations of roughly $12.8 trillion (including the cost of redeeming the Trust Fund). As a result, changes in the program are inevitable.

In making these changes, however, it is particularly important that we consider their impact on the most vulnerable Americans who disproportionately depend on Social Security. For example, the poorest 20 percent of Americans receive nearly all of their retirement income from Social Security, while the wealthiest fifth of Americans receive less than 20 percent of their retirement income from the system. It is also important to understand that it is not just reform that will affect these vulnerable Americans, but so too will a failure to reform the system. Since Social Security currently cannot pay promised benefits, those benefits will eventually have to be reduced by roughly 26 percent, a reduction that will fall heaviest on those who can least afford it.

Chance to Build Wealth

On the other hand, reform, properly structured, can not only protect the poor and vulnerable from these otherwise inevitable benefit cuts, but can actually produce an improved Social Security system that will leave them better off. We can give low income workers a chance to build real inheritable wealth. We can give them an ownership stake in the American economy. And, while maintaining a safety net, we can give them a chance to earn a higher rate of return, leading to higher retirement benefits that would lift millions of seniors out of poverty.

Social Security has elements of both an insurance and a welfare program. It is, in effect, both a retirement and an anti-poverty program. However, in attempting to combine these two functions, it has ended up doing neither particularly well. While much time has been spent discussing Social Security's shortcomings as a retirement program, far less attention has been paid to its inadequacies as an anti-poverty program.

There is no question that the poverty rate among the elderly has declined dramatically in the last half century. As recently as 1959, the poverty rate for seniors was 35.2 percent, more than double the 17 percent poverty rate for the general adult population. Today, it has declined to approximately 10 percent.

Important Antipoverty Program

Clearly Social Security has had a significant impact on this trend. Studies suggest that in the absence of Social Security benefits more than half of seniors would have income below the poverty level. This suggests that receipt of Social Security benefits lifted millions of seniors out of poverty. Moreover, the percentage of elderly in poverty after receiving Social Security benefits has been steadily declining in recent years, indicating the increased importance of Social Security as an anti-poverty remedy.

However, there is a superficiality to this line of analysis. It assumes that any loss of Social Security benefits would not be offset through other sources of income. In other words, it simply takes a retiree's current income and subtracts Social

Security benefits to discover, no surprise, that the total income is now lower and, indeed, frequently low enough to throw the retiree into poverty.

That much should be obvious. Social Security benefits are a substantial component of most retirees' income. It constitutes more than 90 percent of retirement income for one-quarter of the elderly. Nearly half of retirees receive at least half of their income from Social Security. The question, therefore, is not whether the sudden elimination of Social Security income would leave retirees worse off—clearly it would—but whether in the absence of Social Security (or an alternative mandatory savings program) retirees would have changed their behavior to provide other sources of income for their own retirement.

African American Seniors

However, even taking the idea of Social Security as an anti-poverty tool on its own terms, the evidence suggests that the current Social Security is inadequate. After all, despite receiving Social Security benefits, roughly one out of ten seniors still lives in poverty. In fact, the poverty rate among seniors remains slightly higher than that for the adult population as a whole. And, among some subgroups the problem is far worse. For the poverty rate is over 20 percent among elderly women who are never married or widowed and roughly 30 percent among divorced or separated women. African-American seniors are also disproportionately left in poverty. Nearly a third of African-Americans over the age of 65 have incomes below the poverty level.

In addition, lifetime Social Security benefits depend, in part, on longevity. As a result, people with identical earnings histories will receive different levels of benefits depending on how long they live. Individuals who live to be 100 receive far more in benefits than individuals who die at 66. Therefore,

Privatization Would Help African Americans

Although African Americans are disadvantaged under both the current Social Security system and many of the most commonly discussed solutions to the program's future financial crisis, they would be among those who would benefit most from Social Security privatization.

First, by transforming Social Security from a defined-benefit to a defined-contribution plan, privatization would disconnect total benefits from life expectancy. The benefits an individual received would depend on what was paid into the system plus the investment return on those payments, not on how many years the person received benefits.

In addition, individuals who begin work earlier, and therefore contribute for additional years, would earn additional benefits as a result of their contributions.

Moreover, under a privatized system, individuals would have a property right to their Social Security benefits. If a person were to die with money still in his or her retirement account, that money would become part of the estate to be inherited by that person's heirs.

Michael Tanner,
Cato Institute Briefing Paper No. 61,
February 2001.

those groups in our society with shorter life expectancies, such as the poor and African-Americans, are put at a severe disadvantage.

Of course, Social Security does have a progressive benefit formula, whereby low-income individuals receive proportionately higher benefits per dollar paid into the system than do high-income workers. The question, therefore is to what degree shorter life expectancies offset this progressivity.

Using income as the sole criterion, the literature is mixed. Some studies, such as those by Eugene Steuerle and Jan Bakja of the Urban Institute and Dean Leimer of the Social Security Administration conclude that shorter life expectancies diminish but do not completely offset Social Security's progressivity. However, there is a growing body of literature, including studies by Daniel Garrett of Stanford University, the RAND corporation, Jeffrey Liebman, and others that show the progressive benefit formula is completely offset, resulting in redistribution from poor people to wealthy.

Shorter Lives Means Fewer Benefits

The question of Social Security's unfairness to ethnic minorities appears more straightforward, particularly in the case of African-Americans. At all income levels and all ages, African-Americans have shorter life expectancies than do whites. As a result, a black man or woman, earning exactly the same lifetime wages, and paying exactly the same lifetime Social Security taxes, as his or her white counterpart, will likely receive far less in lifetime Social Security benefits.

This disparity has a significant impact on the concentration of wealth in our society. Social Security benefits are not inheritable. A worker can pay Social Security taxes for 30 or 40 years, but if that worker dies without children under the age of 18 or a spouse over the age of 65, none of the money paid into the system is passed on to his heirs. As Cato Senior Fellow Jagadedesh Gokhale, has noted, Social Security essentially forces low-income workers to annuitize their wealth,[1] preventing them from making a bequest of that wealth to their heirs.

---

1. Annuitization means that all contributions into the pension, whether private or public, become property of another party—here the federal government. In exchange the contributor is guaranteed a certain level of income for life.

Moreover, because this forced annuitization applies to a larger portion of the wealth of low income workers than high income workers, it turns inheritance into a "disequalizing force," leading to greater inequality of wealth in America. The wealthy are able to bequeath their wealth to their heirs, while the poor cannot. Indeed, Gokhale and Boston University economist Laurence Kotlikoff estimate that Social Security doubles the share of wealth owned by the richest one percent of Americans.

Substituting Social Security Wealth

Martin Feldstein of Harvard University reaches a similar conclusion. Feldstein suggests that low-income workers substitute "Social Security wealth" in the form of promised future Social Security benefits for other forms of savings. As a result, a greater proportion of a high-income worker's wealth is in fungible [transferable] assets. Since fungible wealth is inheritable, while Social Security wealth is not, this has led to a stable concentration of fungible wealth among a small proportion of the population. Feldstein's work suggests that the concentration of wealth in the United States would be reduced by as much as half if low-income workers were able to substitute real wealth for Social Security wealth.

Properly constructed, a Social Security reform plan including personal accounts can solve these problems. HR [House Resolution] 530, introduced [in 2005 by Texas Congressman Sam] Johnson, provides an excellent example of how this would work. Mr. Johnson's bill would allow younger workers to save and invest their half of the Social Security payroll tax (6.2 percent of wages) through personal accounts. Because workers would own the money in their accounts—which they do not under the current system—that money would be fully inheritable. If they die before retirement, they would be able to pass all the money in their account on to their loved ones; death after retirement would still leave substantial unused portions for their heirs.

And, it is not just future generations who would benefit from this ownership. Personal accounts would give low-income workers a chance to build a nest egg of real wealth for the first time in their lives, giving them a real and personal stake in the economy. As Michael Sherraden of Washington University in St. Louis has shown, ownership can have significant beneficial impact on a variety of social pathologies, not only increasing work effort and the propensity to save, but even reducing crime, drug abuse, school drop out rates, and illegitimacy. Giving people an ownership stake in America—something that HR 530, with its recognition bonds[2] does even more than other personal account plans—could be considered one of the most important anti-poverty proposals we could undertake. . . .

In summation, Social Security reform is inevitable. If we simply fall back on the old ways of raising taxes and cutting benefits, we will significantly harm those most in need. If we do nothing, we end up with a benefit reduction that the poor and vulnerable can ill afford. However, by making personal accounts part of any Social Security reform, we can give low-income workers a chance to build a nest egg of real inheritable wealth. In combination with an enhanced safety net, we can provide vulnerable workers with a new and better Social Security system.

---

2. Recognition bonds recognize the contribution of each individual to the retirement system. In the current pay-as-you-go system, all Social Security payroll taxes (contributions) are put into a single pod of funds.

| "Private accounts would not be a good bet for African Americans."

Social Security Privatization Will Not Help African Americans

William E. Spriggs

Politicians and policy experts regularly suggest privatizing part or all of the Social Security system, as did President George W. Bush in 2005. In the viewpoint that follows, economics professor William E. Spriggs, a senior fellow at the Economic Policy Institute, argues that privatization of the nation's primary social insurance program would bring little benefit to African Americans. Indeed, because their families and children are more reliant than whites on the current Social Security system, he contends that black Americans could be disproportionately hurt by privatization. For this reason, Spriggs believes, the black community must be especially wary of any privatization plans.

As you read, consider the following questions:

1. What occupations were originally excluded from the Social Security program, according to Spriggs?

William E. Spriggs, "Pulling a Fast One? The Facts About Social Security," *Crisis*, vol. 112, March/April 2005, pp. 17–21. Copyright © 2005 Crisis Magazine. All rights reserved. Reproduced by permission of Crisis Publishing Co., the publisher of the magazine of the National Association for the Advancement of Colored People.

2. According to the author, what percentage of black children receive Social Security benefits?

3. According to Spriggs, the average Social Security survivor's benefit is equivalent to a life insurance policy worth how much?

The status of Social Security is dominating the public policy debate. Will our elders have their benefits reduced? Will payments the hip-hop generation is making to the program be available to draw on when it retires? Is [then-president George W.] Bush's plan to privatize Social Security a good idea, and how much will it cost? Do the Democrats have an alternative plan? Questions abound.

Despite all the hype, there is no Social Security "crisis." However, in several decades there may be a shortfall, so it would behoove us to consider some adjustments to the program so that it remains sound.

There are a few basic facts we should all know:

- Social Security is not just a program for retirees, but one that offers a degree of security for families.

- The average age of a Black Social Security beneficiary is 58.

- Roughly one of every 16 African American children—700,000 in all—receives a monthly Social Security check.

What Is Social Security?

Social Security's formal name is the Old Age, Survivors and Disability Insurance (OASDI) program. As the name suggests, it is an insurance program, not a retirement program. The tax that supports the program is called the Federal Insurance Contributions Act (FICA), and the benefits are determined by the Primary Insurance Amount (PIA).

Each pay period when workers contribute to Social Security through their FICA deduction, they are purchasing insurance for their families against loss of income should they become disabled, die or live to old age. Each risk—disability, death and old age—is balanced using the entire American work force as the risk pool; making it "social." Family benefits are determined using only one formula, the PIA, based on a worker's history of earnings. So, from the family's perspective, for a given worker, benefits would be the same whether the worker becomes disabled, dies or retires. And the benefits are "secured" by law.

President Franklin Roosevelt created the push for Social Security in January 1935. On the heels of the economic collapse of the Great Depression, Roosevelt wanted to protect Americans from economic uncertainty created by unemployment, old age and disability and to protect children from being made destitute by life's chances. Congress followed with the drafting of what was called the Economic Security Act, which soon became the Social Security Bill. Roosevelt signed it into law in August 1935. In signing the law, Roosevelt said, "We can never insure one-hundred percent of the population against one-hundred percent of the hazards and vicissitudes of life. But we have tried to frame a law which will give some measure of protection to the average citizen and to his family."

America is different today, but so is Social Security. Indeed, President [John F.] Kennedy commented in 1961, "The Social Security program plays an important part in providing for families, children and older persons in time of stress. But it cannot remain static. Changes in our population, in our working habits and in our standard of living require constant revision."

As originally crafted, Social Security excluded domestics and agricultural workers—effectively excluding much of the African American work force in 1935. Between 1935 and 1975, major changes in the Social Security system made the program progressively more favorable to African Americans. in 1939, benefits were extended to family members so that dependents and survivors were brought into the system, in 1950, coverage was extended to farm and domestic workers.

In 1956, disability benefits were created, first for those ages 50 to 64, and children who became disabled before age 18 were allowed to draw benefits as adults. In 1960, the disability provision was changed to allow disability at any age. In 1961, an early retirement option was created so male workers could retire at age 62. Beginning in 1975, benefits were automatically adjusted to increases in the cost of living, so inflation could not erode their purchasing power. And, in 1977, initial benefit levels were tied to increases in wages so benefits would now be assured of replacing a percentage of a worker's earnings.

Who Benefits from the Program?

Thanks to the aforementioned changes and others over the years, almost 4.8 million African Americans greatly benefit from Social Security. Slightly less than half of African American beneficiaries are retired workers, a little more than 30 percent are family members of retired, disabled or deceased workers, and the remaining almost 20 percent are disabled workers. So while African Americans are slightly less than 12 percent of those who pay into Social Security, they make up 13 percent of those getting survivor benefits, 18 percent of those getting disability benefits and 22 percent of children getting benefits.

Research done by the National Urban League Institute for Opportunity and Equality shows that African American children are four times more likely than White children to be lifted out of poverty by Social Security benefits they receive. The result is that though African American men have a higher death rate in their 40s and 50s, and a much higher disability rate than White men, African Americans pay roughly 9 percent of Social Security taxes and get about 9 percent of Social Security benefits.

A False Claim

African Americans on average have substantially shorter life expectancies than other Americans. Therefore they are short-changed by Social Security.

The first statement is true: on average, African Americans do die younger than other Americans. But the second statement does not follow: there is almost no difference in Social Security's payback by race. There are two reasons for this. First, African Americans on average earn less than other Americans, and Social Security is a substantially better deal for low-wage than high-wage workers. Second, more than a third of Social Security benefits go to disabled workers and survivors of deceased workers. Non-whites make up 19 percent of this group of beneficiaries.

Bernard Wasow,
Century Foundation Social Security Network,
March 1, 2002. www.socsec.org.

And even though African American workers on average pay only 73 percent of the Social Security taxes paid by White workers, African American beneficiaries on average get a benefit that is 81 percent of what White beneficiaries get.

Not All Changes Benefit Blacks

However, all changes in Social Security have not been beneficial to African Americans. The last major changes took place in 1981 and 1983, when the fear that the retirement of the baby boom generation would drive the program into bankruptcy created a Social Security "crisis."

The solutions were to increase revenue—from 5.4 percent of wages from each worker to today's worker contribution of

6.2 percent—and include a series of cuts in benefits, increasing the full retirement age from 65 to 67, stopping benefits for widows with dependent children when the child reached 16 and limiting benefits for surviving students when they graduated from college or reached 21 to when they graduated from high school or reached 19.

But the last two "cost-saving" measures did not address the issue of the baby boom effect. (The baby boom generation will begin drawing retirement benefits soon; however, the share of workers to beneficiaries is shrinking from 3.3 today to roughly 2.2 workers in 25 years to support each beneficiary.)

In addition, the measures negatively affected African Americans disproportionately to Whites because a higher share of African American children (6 percent) than White children (4 percent) receive Social Security benefits. This is an example of why African Americans must pay extreme attention to the details of proposals to change Social Security. . . .

Effects of Privatization

In his State of the Union address in February [2005], President Bush mentioned several ideas that have been proposed by others to cut benefits so Social Security could be put on a path toward long-term stability. He did not say whether he favored any of those proposals. He did, however, put forth an idea that he wants included as part of a new program: privatizing Social Security. . . .

He proposes that workers may borrow one-third of their benefits to fund a limited set of investment options. At retirement, the worker must repay the loan with interest, set by the government at 3 percent interest above the rate of inflation—for 2004 that would mean a 6.3 percent rate of interest—the approximate yield on U.S. Treasury notes.

If participants' earnings from the individual accounts bring them returns higher than the cost of interest on their loan, then they will come out ahead. If not, at retirement they will have to repay the loan to the government using money from their guaranteed Social Security benefit.

President Bush has repeatedly asserted that this innovation would make Social Security a better program for African Americans. On their own, the private accounts would not be a good bet for African Americans. Blacks die younger than Whites, and so far the president has not made clear whether the loan would have to be repaid by surviving heirs. While in the long run stocks may have a higher yield than U.S. Treasury notes, in the short run they often do not do better, and so private accounts could easily lose money. Even though the president promises a program that slowly shifts from stock to bond investments as the worker ages, the untimely death of a worker too heavily in a bearish stock market could hurt his or her survivors' benefits.

The current Social Security benefit formula corrects for several factors of racial discrimination in the labor market that private accounts would exacerbate. First, young African Americans are far less likely to have jobs than are young Whites. For instance, in January 2005, nearly 75 percent of Whites 20 to 29 years old had jobs, compared with about 60 percent of African Americans. With private accounts, savings deposited in early years count much more than later in life because the interest earned on those accounts have more years to compound.

Beyond labor market problems, African Americans need more education to earn the income of less-educated Whites. For instance, in 2003, the median earnings for White high school graduates was $26,518 a year. Yet African Americans needed high school plus some college coursework to get to a median earnings level of $26,129.

Helping Close the Income Gap

Social Security currently considers a worker's 35 highest earning years to calculate their benefit, so the difficulties African

Americans have in their early years do not matter in determining Social Security benefits. And the Social Security benefit formula compensates people with lower earnings by giving them a higher share of their pre-retirement earnings in benefits than higher income workers.

The result is that African American households aged 65 and older have 55 percent of the income of African American households aged 55 to 64, while for Whites, seniors have income that is 47 percent of the pre-retirement age cohort [statistical group]. And the income gap between African American and White households headed by seniors older than 65 is 26 cents on the dollar, the smallest gap for any age group of African American households.

Second, as Christian Weller at the Center for American Progress has pointed out, stocks return their highest yield if you buy when they are low and sell when they are high. But job opportunities for African Americans are more sensitive to changes in the economy than those for other groups, as William Rodgers III at Rutgers University and others have documented. The result is that when the economy is growing, the stock market does well, and African Americans are able to find jobs—enabling people to build their portfolios when the market is high. Then, when the economy slows, and the market is low, African American unemployment jumps, and fewer African Americans are able to put money into the accounts when the market is low. Weller shows this phenomenon would substantially reduce the returns on African Americans' accounts relative to those held by Whites.

No Gain in Inheritable Wealth

Third, President Bush has touted private accounts as a way to create inheritable wealth for African Americans. In that, the president is totally ignoring the value of Social Security's survivor benefits, which on average amount to a $403,000 life insurance policy.

The president's plan requires retirees to buy an annuity—the guaranteed stream of monthly payments that end when you die—with their savings accounts large enough that when combined with their traditional Social Security benefit would lift the worker out of poverty.

However, Dean Baker at the Center for Economic and Policy Research has estimated that after buying such an annuity only the upper half of African American male earners would have enough in their private account to keep some of their savings to leave behind.

Unless African American retirees already had high enough earnings and savings to leave something behind, the private accounts would not add to inheritance for African Americans.

"Privatization negatively impacts the most vulnerable segments of the workforce, especially women."

Privatization of Pension Systems Generally Harms Women

Ross Prizzia

Ross Prizzia is professor of public administration at the University of Hawaii–West Oahu. In the following viewpoint he outlines how women around the world have been affected by privatization of social security systems. Women tend to earn less than men, are less likely to work for an employer with a pension plan, and tend to work fewer years due to bearing and raising children. This means they benefit disproportionately from the wealth redistribution effects of most pay-as-you-go public retirement systems. Prizzia contends that privatization threatens this income boost for elderly women.

As you read, consider the following questions:

1. How many years do women lose (on average) from paid work due to raising children or other types of unpaid caring duties, according to Prizzia?

Ross Prizzia, "An International Perspective of Privatization and Women Workers," *Journal of International Women's Studies*, vol. 7, no. 1, November 2005, pp. 62–66. Reproduced by permission.

2. In the author's opinion, why do women's longer life spans create worries for them when privatization of Social Security is discussed?

3. Which three countries are described by Prizzia as having privatized their pension systems?

The Social Security Commission's 2001–2002 and 2004–2005 proposals to privatize the Social Security system in the United States threaten to severely weaken the guaranteed benefits on which women depend. For example, establishment of private accounts would require deep cuts in disability and survivor benefits. Many of those who need Social Security most could not afford to buy comparable private disability or life insurance. In contrast to Social Security's guaranteed lifetime retirement income, the Commission's proposed private accounts may not provide adequate lifetime income because no allowances are made for long life, health costs, or the volatility of the stock market. The plan fails to account for Social Security's protections against inflation and its progressive benefit formula, which are particularly important to women because they live longer and have lower lifetime earnings than men.

The statistics on Social Security in the United States show that women comprise:

1. over half of Social Security beneficiaries,

2. over two-fifths of the beneficiaries of disabled worker benefits,

3. 99 percent of the spouses receiving Social Security benefits,

4. 99 percent of the non-disabled surviving beneficiaries, and

5. 98 percent of the dually entitled; that is, persons entitled to benefits as retired workers and as spouses.

Women Depend on Social Security

Widowed, divorced, and never-married women, in particular, depend heavily on Social Security which accounts for half or more of the income of nearly three-fourths of non-married female recipients. For one in four, it is the only source of income. Approximately 60 percent of Social Security recipients age 65 and older, and roughly 72 percent of beneficiaries age 85 and older are women. Women rely heavily on Social Security as a source of income in old age in part because they are less likely to be covered by an employer-sponsored pension plan. Social Security comprises a larger portion of their total retirement income; twenty-seven percent of women age 65 and older count on Social Security for 90 percent of their income.

Because women, on average, earn less than men, they rely on Social Security's progressive benefit structure to ensure that they have an adequate income in retirement. The progressive benefit structure means that lower earners have a higher proportion of their pre-retirement earnings replaced by Social Security than higher-earning workers. This is especially important since women lose an average of 14 years of earnings due to time out of the workforce to raise children or to care for ailing parents or spouses, and they generally have a higher incidence of part-time employment. In addition, women live 6 to 8 years longer than men, so they must make retirement savings stretch over longer periods of time. Consequently, women depend on Social Security's life-long benefits, which are fully protected against inflation. No privatization proposal can prevent individual account balances from being eroded by inflation. Social Security resolves this problem by adjusting benefits each year through an automatic cost-of-living adjustment (COLA) that is tied to the annual increase in the Consumer Price Index, the official measure of inflation. This feature of Social Security along with other benefits would be lost with the privatization of Social Security.

The American Association of University Women (AAUW) strongly opposes private accounts in place of Social Security benefits, which are the sole, guaranteed source of income for many elderly women. The AAUW contends that the current Social Security system contains many benefits that must be maintained, including full cost of living adjustments, a progressive benefit formula, spousal and widow benefits, and disability and survivor benefits. The AAUW advocates that any Social Security reform must maintain these guaranteed benefits and consider the inequity of pension benefits and retirement security for women.

Increasing Gender Inequality

In Chile, a 1999 study showed that the new privately managed pension system increased gender inequalities. Women are worse off than they were under the old pay-as-you-go system of social security, in which the calculation of benefits for men and women did not differ and women could obtain pensions with fewer requirements than men. Currently, benefits are calculated according to individuals' contributions and levels of risk. Such factors as women's longer life expectancy, earlier retirement age, and lower rates of labor-force participation, lower salaries, and other disadvantages in the labor market are directly affecting their accumulation of funds in individual retirement accounts, leading to lower pensions, especially for poorer women. The 1999 study sparked a debate on a critical but neglected aspect of the privatization of the social security system in Chile: its effects on the welfare of women. Previous studies of social welfare in Latin America have either ignored or paid insufficient attention to the gender dimension of inequality and currently, when several countries in the region are striving to reform their social security systems, many questions relevant to the social protection of women remain unanswered. For example, is the social security system compensating for the disadvantages that women experience in the labor market? To what extent are social benefits for older women reflecting conflicts between women's roles as workers and caregivers? These questions have become more pressing in the last decade because more women are qualifying for retirement pensions due to increases in their participation in the paid labor force.

In his evaluation of the Chilean privatization initiative, Peter Diamond concluded that, "We have come to think of privatization as a route to greater efficiency and lower costs. Thus, perhaps the most surprising aspect of the Chilean reform is the high cost of running a privatized social security system, higher than the 'inefficient' system that is replaced." In theory, advocates predicted that competition among financial investment organizations would keep costs down. In practice, however, this has not happened. While high fees impact both men and women, it is a serious problem that is especially troublesome for women, as illustrated by the Chilean and other countries' experiences. In 1996, six out of the 15 authorized investment companies in Chile charged a fixed rate fee for each contribution made by a worker. This fixed rate fee had a greater impact on lower paid workers, affecting more women than men. According to [the Social Security Administration's] Barbara Kritzer, "even though the average fee varies by only a few percentage points, the lower earner continues to have to pay at a higher contribution rate than does the higher earner."

European Privatization Hurt Women

In 1999, Sweden dramatically altered its pension law. Similar to U.S. Social Security, Sweden's old system paid out a defined benefit based on salary and years of employment, using contributions from current workers to support retirees. The new plan includes mandatory individual accounts. Of the 18.5 percent payroll tax that workers set aside for retirement, 16 percent goes to a defined benefit program. The other 2.5 percent must be put into individual investment accounts. Workers

Women Benefit from Social Security

The Social Security system is progressive in that lower-wage earners receive a higher percentage benefit than higher-wage earners do. The system returns a greater percentage of pre-retirement earnings to a lower-wage worker than to a higher-wage worker. Women who are low-wage workers receive back more benefits in relation to past earnings than do high-wage earners.

In 2007, the median earnings of working-age women who worked full-time, year-round were $35,000, compared to $45,000 for men.

Social Security Administration Factsheet,
www.socialsecurity.gov.

choose from some 650 funds or accept the government-managed "default" fund. The government launched the private account plan with a massive public relations campaign that encouraged participants to select their own portfolios, and according to Annika Sunden, an economist at the Center for Retirement Research at Boston College, "There was tremendous emphasis that now you have the chance to affect your benefit in a positive way. People were very enthusiastic, but then the market dropped and most people, women in particular, lost money and have not recuperated." In the final analysis, the default fund returned 7.2 percent, outperforming the defined benefit program. When the plan began, 68 percent of participants chose their own portfolio. In 2001 that number decreased to 20 percent of new participants and by 2003 it had dropped to less than 10 percent.

Similarly in Great Britain, in 1986, the [Margaret] Thatcher government offered to let people divert part of their social security taxes into a personal investment account similar to a 401(k). For help in designing the plan, the government turned to the insurance industry, the main source of long-term investment products in Britain. The competition to sell pension investment products to the public was intense. Products were numerous and complicated, and few people could understand them. Fees and costs often were not fully disclosed by agents, who could pocket a portion of the first few years' sales. Rules were poorly designed and rarely enforced. More money was lost by taxes being diverted to private accounts than the government would have paid out in entitlements, and the government lost a 1.58 billion-pound surplus in the National Insurance Fund. Worst of all, many workers, and especially women, who switched from good company pension plans to private investments ended up with a poorer retirement. Since the private investments required upfront charges and commissions, plus annual administration fees, there was often little on which investment returns could accumulate. People began to realize that they could no longer be certain that investment returns would equal what they had given up by switching to private accounts. Later, after the stock market crash in 2001, even the insurance industry began advising customers to return to the government system. In 2004 alone, 500,000 people abandoned private pensions and moved back into the traditional government plan. . . . In dealing with its problems, the U.K. [United Kingdom] Pensions Commission concluded that there are only four possible solutions: cut state retirement benefits, increase taxes, increase personal savings or delay retirement. Noting that there is no political support for the first choice, the commission determined that each of the three other choices, on its own, would be too painful and that only some combinations could work. According to U.K. Pension Commission Chairman Adair Turner, a vice president of Merrill Lynch in London and the former director general of the U.K.'s biggest business lobbying group, "There are no other choices."

Considering Women's Needs

The impact on the adequacy of social security benefits provided under privatization schemes in most countries is a bigger issue for women because they are more negatively affected by the basic differences between the typical social security scheme (i.e., "defined benefit" plans) and the typical privatized scheme (i.e., "defined contribution" plans). Lessons from the privatization of social security in Chile, Sweden, and Great Britain and the widespread opposition by women to similar proposals in the United States, should stimulate scholars, policy makers, and the general public to more critically scrutinize the losses and gains that accompany social security privatization. The need to incorporate gender variables in designing and implementing policy changes is clearly evident.

Worldwide research studies on the effectiveness of privatization over the last ten years provide ample evidence that when the balance of social and economic indicators are not present, a privatized activity which appears to have a successful outcome may be only short-term or misleading. Moreover, when judged in the broader context, the overall successful financial outcome of the privatization activity may have done more harm than good in the long-term to important human and social dimensions of the affected community.

Privatization activities are expanding relatively unchecked into traditionally public sector domains on national and international levels. There is concern that privatization negatively impacts the most vulnerable segments of the workforce, especially women workers. The economic plight of female workers is but one of a number of increasingly disturbing effects of privatization as it continues to grow globally in scope and role. The proposals to privatize social security and more health and social services, continue at a rapid pace, and other essential public services are forthcoming. More than ever, the caution to consider the social consequences of privatization that threaten basic social justice and human rights ... must be taken seriously if there is to be any hope for an equitable and peaceful global community.

> *"Personal accounts would increase the incentive to work by allowing a woman to own and control a portion of her Social Security contributions."*

Private Retirement Accounts Would Be Fairer than Social Security to Women

Leanne Abdnor

Leanne Abdnor, a nationally recognized expert on Social Security, was a member of President George W. Bush's Commission to Strengthen Social Security. She makes the case, in the viewpoint that follows, that the Social Security system is based on a form of family that was common in the 1930s, when the system was created. These assumptions are outmoded today, she contends. More women wait longer to marry, or never marry, and more are divorced. The current system gives these women fewer benefits than women in "traditional" marriages. According to Abdnor, only privatization can correct these inequities.

Leanne Abdnor, "Social Security Choice for the 21st-Century Woman," Social Security Paper, no. 33, February 24, 2004, pp. 111–112, 120–123, 125–126. Copyright © 2004 by Cato. Republished with permission of Cato Institute, conveyed through Copyright Clearance Center, Inc.

As you read, consider the following questions:

1. Under proposals for personal retirement accounts, what percentage of wages would be diverted from contributions from the government system into private accounts, according to Abdnor?

2. Under the current system, at what age is a widow able to receive a Social Security survivor's benefit, according to the author?

3. As noted by Abdnor, what position do most mainstream women's groups take toward Social Security privatization?

Although most women work today, Social Security's original benefit structure—designed for a time when the single-earner family was the norm—is largely unchanged. And although Social Security still provides partial protection against poverty, spousal and survivors' benefit regulations now clash with women's changed roles and options in our society.

Indeed, Social Security's outmoded benefit structure is increasingly a source of discrimination and unfairness, pitting women against women. Among those adversely affected are millions of married women who have joined the workforce and many divorced and single women who are providing for themselves and their dependents. Social Security's 1935-era benefit structure means that the benefits of wealthier single-earner couples are subsidized by everyone else, including dual-earning couples, who also often receive disproportionately lower benefits. Furthermore, many divorced women are left with no claim to spousal or survivors' benefits.

Moreover, the discrimination and unfairness in today's system are likely to increase as Social Security wrestles with impending insolvency. After all, Social Security will begin running deficits in just 15 years [from 2004].

Both the system's financing problems and the inequities in its benefit structure can be resolved by allowing younger workers, including younger women, the choice of privately investing at least a portion of their Social Security taxes through personal retirement accounts. Not only would personal accounts help to solve Social Security's financial problems by taking advantage of the higher returns available to private capital investment, they would give women true ownership and control of their retirement income and create a benefit structure far more tailored to the needs of the modern family. . . .

Allowing Personal Accounts

Given Social Security's financial crisis, it is not surprising that many proposals for Social Security reform are currently being debated in Washington. But the traditional ways of tinkering with Social Security's financing, raising taxes or cutting benefits, would do nothing to fix the inequities discussed above. However, one reform would both help to restore Social Security to solvency *and* make the program fairer for women and today's families: allowing workers to invest at least part of their Social Security taxes through individual accounts.

Proposals for personal retirement accounts range from diverting just 2 percent of wages to the full 10 percent of wages currently paid for Old-Age and Survivors Insurance into an individually owned and controlled account. In addition, some proposals are progressive in nature, allowing low-wage workers to divert and invest a greater percentage of wages than high-wage workers. Because women are a large proportion of those in the lower-wage group, many women would have the choice of investing more of their income. . . .

[A] study done by [economist] Marianne Baxter of Boston University suggests that, indeed, "women would have more to gain, compared with men, from a reformed Social Security system that would permit investment of retirement funds in other forms of financial assets." Personal accounts would eliminate the distortions that exist under the current system that favors single-earner couples.

Personal accounts would help a woman who is part of a two-earner couple because she would be proportionately rewarded for her time in the workplace. Whatever funds a woman contributed to her individual account would belong to her. In contrast, as stated earlier, with the current spousal benefit, many working wives receive no extra benefits at the margin. More work doesn't necessarily equal higher benefits. Personal accounts would increase the incentive to work by allowing a woman to own and control a portion of her Social Security contributions.

Under the current system, a widow is not entitled to a Social Security survivor's benefit until she reaches age 60 unless she has dependent children. However, if her husband had had a personal retirement account, the funds in the account would be part of his estate and inheritable by his wife. She could use those funds to get additional training, start a small business, or in whatever way she chose to help her adjust to a different lifestyle.

Under a system of individual accounts, a couple could choose among different distribution methods. The couple could convert the personal account into an inflation-adjusted annuity for life or leave it in safe investments and take programmed withdrawals in retirement. In the latter case, a widow would be entitled to all the remaining funds that had accumulated in the account. If the couple chose, they could leave the funds in the account to their children, grandchildren, or others. As the President's Commission to Strengthen Social Security states: "Unlike Social Security, assets held in personal retirement accounts can be bequeathed to heirs if the account owner dies before retirement. In this way, wealth accumulation in the family need not be cut short with the death of the primary earner."

Social Security Favors Men

Although the Social Security system is gender neutral on its face, it produces some financial outcomes that place women at a disadvantage in retirement compared with men.

- The employment patterns of women, characterized by fewer years in the labor force, lower earnings, and more frequent job changes, translate into lower Social Security benefits.

- The dual-entitlement rules of the system often impose a penalty on wives and widows of two-earner couples.

- The loss of up to 50 percent of a couple's benefit at the husband's death throws every fifth widow into poverty.

Ekaterina Shirley and Peter Spiegler, Cato Institute Social Security Project Paper No. 12, July 20, 1998.

Private investment through personal retirement accounts would bring a better rate of return than can be provided by the current Social Security system. Higher rates of return translate directly to higher benefits. Moreover, single women without dependents—a growing demographic group in our society—who die before retirement forfeit all of the money they have paid in taxes to Social Security. However, if those women had had the option of a personal retirement account, they could pass the account on to a relative, partner, or other person of their choice.

Personal retirement accounts would provide a fair solution for all divorcees by establishing property rights in spousal benefits regardless of the duration of the marriage. At divorce, the accumulations in a couple's accounts during their marriage would be split and added to their individual accounts regardless of the length of the marriage. Thus, from "day one" of a marriage, a woman would own wealth. . . .

Women's Right to Choose

Women—and to their credit, women's advocacy groups—have broken down many walls that for centuries kept women dependent and politically unrepresented. As a society, we have come to recognize that women are as capable as men of making decisions about their own lives.

There is no longer a legal barrier to women independently achieving positions of fame, power, or wealth. Women can expect to choose where to live, what work to do, what to study, where to travel, and with whom to partner. They can choose whether to marry, divorce, conceive children, travel the world, run for public office, and so on.

It is ironic, therefore, that the largest women's advocacy groups in the United States are flatly opposed to giving women the right to have a choice between the existing insolvent system and one that gives them more control and ownership of their retirement funds. After all, this is, ultimately, a question of choice. Under all the major reform proposals, individual accounts would be *voluntary*. A woman could choose, if she wished, to continue to direct all of her Social Security contributions to the current government system. But she would also have the choice of directing part of her taxes to an individual account.

This position of women's rights organizations—opposing the expansion of women's rights and women's freedom to choose—is strangely inconsistent with the stated goals of those organizations. . . .

Reform Is Inevitable

Social Security reform is inevitable. Given the program's huge unfunded liabilities, changes will have to be made. In making them, we should recognize that our society has dramatically changed since the 1930s and Social Security's original benefit structure has not. As a result, Social Security's benefit structure has become increasingly unfair to millions of working women. The Social Security taxes of working women who are married subsidize, in large measure, the free spousal benefits granted to wealthier married women who do not work outside the home. Likewise, divorced and single working women, many of whom are raising children, are disadvantaged under traditional Social Security. As [researchers] Rochelle Stanfield and Corrina Nicolaou of the Urban Institute write, "Unless the program is adjusted to reflect the reality of today's families, important segments of the aging population—particularly widows, divorcees, other unmarried women, and minorities—face an increasingly uncertain future."

Periodical Bibliography

The following articles have been selected to supplement the diverse views presented in this chapter.

Barbara D. Bovbjerg	"Social Security Reform: Issues for Disability and Dependent Benefits," *GAO Reports*, November 26, 2007. www.gao.gov.
Kim Clark	"Mythbuster," *U.S. News and World Report*, January 23, 2006.
James K. Galbraith	"The Parent Trap," *Mother Jones*, May/June, 2005.
Mary Katharine Ham	"Social Security and the Single Girl," *Human Events*, March 15, 2005.
Clover Hope	"NAACP Slams President's Plan for Social Security," *New York Amsterdam News*, February 24, 2005.
Patricia P. Martin and David A. Weaver	"Social Security: A Program and Policy History," *Social Security Bulletin*, March 2005.
Ruth Rosen	"Old Women in the Cold," *Nation*, April 11, 2005.
Daniel Schorr	"Family Insurance," *New Leader*, May 2005.
Alexander Strand and Kalman Rupp	"Disabled Workers and the Indexing of Social Security Benefits," *Social Security Bulletin*, December 2007.
Judie Svihula	"Political Economy, Moral Economy and the Medicare Modernization Act of 2003," *Journal of Sociology and Social Welfare*, March 2008.
USA Today (magazine)	"Outdated Laws Hurt Women," August 2006.
Victoria L. Valentine	"Reform Nation," *Crisis*, March/April 2005.

CHAPTER 4

How Do Other Countries Approach Social Security?

Chapter Preface

The United States is not the only country facing difficulties with its pension system. Around the world populations are aging; countries face the prospect of fewer workers footing the bill for expanding numbers of retirees. Australia has approached this problem through the partial privatization of its pension system. As a relatively rich nation Australia is comparable to the United States. Its experience with private pensions, instituted in its "Superannuation Guarantee" legislation of 1992, may offer applicable lessons for the United States.

In Australia, 9 percent of workers' wages are set aside by employers and are invested in private accounts owned by each individual. Workers are free to contribute additional money to these accounts. To encourage this extra retirement saving, the government offers tax credits for these additional contributions. In addition to the private accounts, Australia has a minimum "safety net" payment which goes to retirees if their retirement income is under a certain threshold.

Daniel Mitchell and Robert P. O'Quinn of the conservative Heritage Foundation wrote in 1998 that savings in retirement accounts had more then doubled since the system of private accounts was begun in 1992. As privatization proponents they conclude:

> Privatization has been a huge success in Australia: Workers will be able to retire with higher incomes, the government has significantly reduced long-term budget pressures, and the economy will benefit by a dramatic increase in savings. . . . Because Australia is in many ways politically and demographically similar to the United States, American policy makers would be well advised to learn the lessons of Australia's successful reforms.

However, later analyses of Australia's system of individual retirement accounts have not been so upbeat. Economists have shown that the high costs of administering private systems such as Australia's lessen retirees' final returns on investments by fifteen to thirty percent. According to a 2004 report by Steven Sass of Boston College:

> Individual account programs are expensive to administer, especially for small accounts and small employers. Financial planning to manage the investment of lump sum distributions, to reduce taxation, and to increase Age Pension entitlements, is thus a large and rapidly growing industry—and presents significant additional cost in the operation of Australia's national retirement income system.

Australia's financial industry has profited from their management of Superannuation funds. However, "fraud and incompetence have resulted in losses by investors, often with no possibility of recouping the lost financial benefits," according to economics professor James Schulz. Schulz also questions whether the Australian case is comparable to the United States. The Australian government offers low income retirees a series of benefits, such as subsidies for rent, communication and transportation costs. The United States lacks similar programs and thus low income retirees would be more at risk if the United States were to switch to an Australian-style, partially privatized system.

As can be seen, there is debate over the effectiveness of privatization in Australia. And of course Australia is not the only country that has experimented with pension system reform. Chile and the United Kingdom are two others whose experiences may be useful to American policy-makers as they draft Social Security reform plans. The following chapter presents differing viewpoints as to how privatized pension systems have fared in these countries.

> *"As British social insurance pensions de-clined, the only way to assure the eld-erly an adequate income was through a means-tested welfare program."*

Britain Is Forced to Supplement Its Privatized Pension System

Alicia H. Munnell and Steven A. Sass

Alicia H. Munnell is the director of the Center for Retirement Research at Boston College, and Steven A. Sass is associate direc-tor for research. In the following viewpoint, the two economists argue that the privatization of pensions has backfired in Britain, where workers were given incentives to "carve out" money from government-sponsored pension programs and invest in indi-vidual accounts—an approach advocated by the United States Social Security Advisory Council. Unfortunately, many private savings plans have not prospered, and to prevent a rise in pov-erty among the elderly the British government now must supple-ment private savings with a form of welfare.

Alicia Haydock Munnell and Steven A. Sass, *Social Security and the Stock Market: How the Pursuit of Market Magic Shapes the System*. Kalamazoo, MI: W.E. Upjohn Institute for Employment Research, 2006, pp. 127–142. Copyright © 2006 W.E. Upjohn Institute for Employment Research. Reproduced by permission.

As you read, consider the following questions:

1. What two factors caused Britain to move toward a private pension system in 1979, according to the authors?

2. According to Munnell and Sass, what is the level of poverty pegged at in the United Kingdom?

3. What do workers give up in return for being allowed to invest part of social insurance contributions into individual private savings accounts, as reported by the authors?

By the end of the 1970s, the United Kingdom had created a retirement income system quite similar to that in the United States. Its two social insurance programs, the flat Basic State Pension and SERPS [State Earnings-Related Pension Scheme], together would have produced benefits very close to those provided by the U.S. Social Security program. Britain also had a robust employer pension institution, similar to that in the United States. A major difference was that the British government allowed, indeed encouraged, employers to "contract out" of SERPS and provide the public earnings-related benefit through their equity-funded pension plan.

The UK System's Reform

In response to a change of government in 1979 and to the growing awareness of the impending demographic transition, the United Kingdom reformed its system along the lines of the [United States Social Security] Advisory Council carve-out approach. It sharply cut public pensions, both the Basic State Pension and SERPS, and shifted an increasing portion of the government's diminished old-age income responsibilities to the private sector. Contracting out had already established the principal of private retirement plans assuming social security obligations, with those plans funded with contributions carved out of the payroll tax and invested in equities. The government now encouraged workers to contract out of SERPS using individual retirement savings accounts. At the same time, the government-guaranteed Basic State Pension was falling to just 15 percent of the national average earnings by the end of the twentieth century and is projected to be just 7 percent by the middle of the twenty-first century.

British employers, like those in the United States, are also withdrawing from traditional defined-benefit plans. The departure came later in Britain and for somewhat different reasons. But, by the beginning of the twenty-first century, private sector employers are closing their defined-benefit plans to new workers and offering, at best, individual account programs where workers bear most of the funding responsibilities and all of the risks. Thus, the great majority of those who contract out of SERPS (roughly half the workforce) will soon be in individual account type programs. So, like American workers under a carve-out reform, British workers are increasingly dependent on sharply reduced government pensions and accumulations in individual retirement accounts.

The British experience illustrates the high cost of administering and regulating accounts carved out of the payroll tax. Most U.S. carve-out proposals would improve on the British design by using the government to collect and administer accounts with small balances. The cost of selling and administering individual accounts, even well above the "small balance" threshold, is nevertheless high. The British mis-selling scandal also illustrates costs created by the vulnerability of carve-out designs to abuse and error.[1] The British experience also illustrates the difficulties carve-out designs encounter in defining regulatory rules on matters such as annuitization and inflation-proofing—difficulties that are costly to overcome.

1. In 1988 the British government's publicity about new private pension plans misled people into taking money out of employer pension plans and investing it in under-performing private financial products.

Administrative Costs of Private Pension Savings Plans Sharply Reduce Assets Available for Retirement

Pension System	Annual Administrative Costs	Percent Reduction in Assets at Retirement
Social Security	$11 per participant	2%
Federal Thrift Savings Plan	$25 per participant	5%
Mutual funds (average)	1.09% of assets	23%
Private defined contribution plans		
Large plans	$24 per participant .8% of assets	21%
Small plans	$60 per participant 1% of assets	30%

Data Source: Congressional Budget Office (2003)

TAKEN FROM: Alicia Haydock Munnell and Steven A. Sass, *Social Security and the Stock Market: How the Pursuit of Market Magic Shapes the System*. Kalamazoo, MI: W.E. Upjohn Institute for Employment Research, 2006.

Welfare for the Elderly

Another lesson from the U.K experience is that the "adequacy" of old-age pensions is more of a "relative" than an "absolute" concept—that is, notions of adequacy are tied to a moving social norm, not a static basket of necessities. Britain price-indexed the Basic State Pension in 1980, in effect defining the basic pension as the basket of goods and services that could be purchased by the Basic State Pension in 1980, which was then 25 percent of average earnings. Britain's welfare system, however, had long pegged poverty as income less than about 20 percent of average earnings, a moving social norm. Both Conservative and Labor governments had used means-tested programs to assure the elderly an income above that threshold amount, pegged to incomes in the economy at large.

As British social insurance pensions declined, the only way to assure the elderly an adequate income was through a means-tested welfare program, but such programs reduce incentives to work and save. To counter the moral hazard created by means-testing, Britain introduced the Pension Credit with a tapered withdrawal rate. Because of the taper, half the elderly population became eligible for means-tested benefits. The proportion will rise as the Basic State Pension continues to decline relative to earnings, since the welfare benchmark keeps pace with earnings growth. By midcentury, three-quarters of the elderly should thus be eligible for means-tested benefits at any point in time and a greater proportion at some point in their lives. The British experience thus illustrates how means-tested programs can rapidly expand through the introduction of a taper designed to counteract moral hazard.

Guaranteed Social Security benefits are especially vulnerable to falling below socially acceptable norms and triggering an expansion of means-testing under a carve-out reform. In the first instance, carve-out proposals reduce Social Security benefits to fit within the program's current resources. Many carve-out proposals do this through price-indexing or some other mechanism that does not assure the elderly an income that will likely be seen as adequate. All carve-out proposals then allow workers to divert a portion of their social insurance contributions into an individual retirement savings account but require in exchange a reduction in their Social Security benefits. Even if a carve-out reform retains an adequate initial benefit, workers who elect the individual account option will generally bring their remaining guaranteed benefit well below the adequacy threshold. The only way to assure such workers an adequate income is through a means-tested program. The British experience suggests that a broad take-up of the individual account option, with a reduction in guaranteed benefits below the socially acceptable level of adequacy, could quickly lead to a major expansion of means-testing that could make the elderly, on the whole, a welfare-dependent population. To avoid this outcome, the British government is now considering major reform of its retirement income system that would abandon the carve-out design.

Privatization's Unexpected Effects

The carve-out approach as implemented in the United Kingdom produced sharply lower guaranteed social insurance benefits, the privatization of much of the nation's diminished retirement income system, increased reliance on individual retirement income planning, and a major expansion of means testing. The goal was to reduce dependence on the state and increase reliance on individual initiative and private financial markets. However, retirement income systems emerged throughout the industrial world because people generally proved themselves incapable of preparing for their own old age. Many people have a myopic view when trading consumption today for consumption in the future. In addition, many people simply lack the information and investment channels they need to accumulate and protect their savings for retirement. The British experience suggests that this original incapacity has not been overcome. If given the latitude, workers will save too little, mishandle the risks and complexities of retirement income planning, and require an extensive safety net. Thus, the outcome of sharp social insurance cutbacks and expanded privatization—in the United States as in Britain—is likely to be just the opposite of what its proponents desire.

> *"The current UK pension system allows individuals an extremely large amount of choice over how much, and in what form, to save privately for retirement."*

Britain Should Not Abandon Pension Privatization

James Banks, Richard Blundell, Richard Disney, and Carl Emmerson

In the viewpoint that follows, four economists with expertise in pension and retirement policy make the case that the United Kingdom's retirement system, which increasingly relies on individual retirement accounts, is not in crisis. The authors acknowledge that some low-income retirees must depend on "means tested" benefits from the government which are a form of welfare for those who have finished their careers. Yet they point out that middle-income workers have been putting money away in private pensions. The economists suggest limited changes to the system; for example, better financial education could improve workers' ability to invest wisely, the authors maintain.

James Banks, Richard Blundell, Richard Disney, and Carl Emmerson, "'Conclusions,' Retirement, Pensions and the Adequacy of Saving: A Guide to the Debate," *Briefing Note No. 29*, Institute for Fiscal Studies, October 2002, pp. 38–40. Copyright © Institute for Fiscal Studies, 2002. Reproduced by permission.

As you read, consider the following questions:

1. According to the authors, what two strategies are possible to maintain levels of retirement income in aging societies?

2. For which types of households do the authors suggest it might be "rational" to rely on the British government's means-tested benefits in retirement, rather than on savings?

3. How has the number of individuals receiving disability benefits changed in the last two decades in the United Kingdom, according to the authors?

The facts that the state pension system is becoming relatively less generous for those not on means-tested benefits, that employers are shifting from defined benefit to defined contribution pension schemes and that life expectancies are increasing have all been put forward as reasons why the UK pension system is in crisis. Even if these phenomena are now happening at an increasing rate, it is important to note that none of them is actually new. The level of social assistance available to pensioners has typically been more generous than the basic state pension. Coverage of defined benefit schemes has been in decline since the mid-1980s. Continued increases in life expectancies are hardly a surprise. But the key issue remains a relevant one, and can be boiled down to the question 'How can we at least maintain post-retirement levels of income while the population continues to age?' Being able to do this seems likely to necessitate either growing levels of retirement saving (either individually or collectively through employers or the state) or longer working lives, or a combination of both.

Private Pensions May Be Adequate

This might not be a problem for government policy. The current UK pension system allows individuals an extremely large amount of choice over how much, and in what form, to save privately for retirement. While there are a significant and growing number of retired people in receipt of means-tested benefits, many working-age individuals will want to save, and are saving, for their retirement. Coverage of private pensions across the earnings distribution does not look inappropriate, and the majority of middle earners already have some form of private pension. Many of those middle earners who do not save in a private pension appear to have sensible reasons for choosing not to do so. Moreover, those with less than £1,500 [about $2,500] in financial assets who also have neither a private pension nor any housing equity tend to be either young or in the bottom half of the (age-specific) income distribution or both. This seems reasonable. Given the paucity of available data, it is currently extremely difficult to assert confidently that individuals are not saving enough. Better data on individuals' liquid financial assets, their housing wealth, their pension wealth and also their debts would be an extremely useful aid to policy-making in this area.

It is of interest to look at individuals' current levels of financial assets and calculate whether there is a 'gap' between the saving that they are currently doing and the amount that they would need to save to reach a target level of income. It should be noted, though, that evidence of a 'gap' does not necessarily answer the question as to what, if anything, the government should do. Saving behaviour and retirement plans will change in the light of changing circumstances, and individuals may automatically adjust their behaviour if the 'savings gap' has arisen as a result of events that were unforeseen when they made their original plans—for example, if the stock market or their pension over- or under-performed compared with their expectations, or if their labour market experiences differed from what they had initially expected. Furthermore, even if no 'savings gap' were identified, there might still be valid reasons for policy changes—for example, if the

British Pension Privatization

Under the British system of social security, a first tier pays a flat-rate basic pension, and a second tier pays pension benefits based on earnings while in the workforce. All eligible employees are entitled to a safety net Basic State Pension, but they also have a choice: remain in an American-style government pension program called the State Earnings Related Pension Scheme (SERPS) or divert a specified portion of their payroll taxes (known as "national insurance contributions") into a private company-based plan or personal pension plan. In this second tier, British employees must be enrolled either in SERPS or an approved private pension plan. If they opt out ("contract out") of SERPS, they give up that portion of their government benefit when they retire, but they also can receive a bigger and better pension with higher returns on their private investments. Workers may contract back into SERPS, with certain restrictions, it they are unhappy with the private option.

Louis D. Enoff and Robert E. Moffit,
Heritage Foundation Backgrounder, *no. 1133,*
August 6, 1997.

government wanted to redistribute different amounts towards different groups of pensioners.

Saving Not Always Appropriate

It is also important not to take low incomes in retirement as evidence of inadequate retirement saving per se. Many households with low retirement incomes will have had low lifetime incomes, and retirement saving may not have been an appropriate activity for them. Means-tested benefits replace a large fraction of earned income when such households retire, and in this situation, particularly given consumption needs that are high relative to income, a reliance on government-provided retirement income may well be 'rational'. Therefore, if it is felt that individuals are not making appropriate saving decisions, then it is important to be clear about why these decisions are not appropriate. In the previous case, individuals are making sensible decisions based on their own circumstances, but there may be a feeling that, perhaps due to the increased reliance on means-tested benefits, these decisions are not optimal from society's point of view. This will depend on how much these individuals would have saved if means-tested benefits were less generous. Another possibility is that individuals are not making sensible saving decisions even from their own perspective. This could be due to the complexities of the UK pension and financial systems. More financial education may well have an important role to play in aiding better saving decisions.

Improving the information that individuals have at their disposal is hindered further by the fact that past experience has shown that the next 'radical' pension reform is never likely to be far away. There have been a large number of pension reforms over the last 20 or so years, many of which have had the effect of adding new complexities. New reforms that add new parts to the pension system have tended to try to avoid creating immediate losers and hence they typically leave a long transition to the 'reformed' system. This has the advantage of a more stable regime for those who are nearer to retirement but often creates a more complex pensions environment for younger individuals.

Improving Work Incentives

This Briefing Note has described various factors that must be considered before a view of appropriate pension policy can be formed. The alternative to working-age individuals consuming less today in order to consume more in their retirement is for them to work for longer. Given the reductions in employment rates among older men and the phenomenal increase in the number of individuals claiming disability benefits over the last 20 years, the government should certainly examine whether reforms could be made that improve work incentives. Final salary defined benefit schemes typically provide individuals nearing retirement with a strong incentive either to work full-time or to retire. The shift from these schemes, in conjunction with increasing numbers of individuals approaching retirement with personal pensions, will reduce the numbers faced with this distortion. This should lead to an increase in more flexible working patterns with more individuals choosing to withdraw gradually from the labour market by working part-time. While this might lead to individuals working for longer, it is also possible that individuals will choose to withdraw partially from the labour market at an earlier age than they would have done.

The other strategy that the government should consider is whether appropriate policies can be used to stimulate employment amongst older workers. On the one hand, . . . with the notable exception of Sweden, employment rates among older workers are actually relatively high in the UK compared with other European countries. On the other hand, however, the data also show that employment rates among older women are higher in the USA than in the UK, and that Japan has higher employment rates among both older men and older women. In addition, employment rates among men in the UK are also much lower than they have been previously. The evidence we have presented has shown that many of the older workers not in employment are on some form of disability benefit. In the short run, it may be hard to move such workers into employment, but in the medium term and beyond, reforms that reduce the flow onto such benefits would very likely increase participation rates among older men in particular.

Financial Education

As is clear from the above, many unanswered research questions will be key to outcomes in the future. These include: Can and will the labour market absorb more older workers? What are the consumption needs of older households? To what extent will individual behaviours (at either the saving or the retirement margin) adjust to meet the pressures of retirement income provision in an ageing population? The private and increasingly individual pension provision approach being taken in the UK adds an extra piece to the puzzle—information provision. Financial education and the simplicity and stability of the planning environment become key to individuals being able to implement their financial plans for retirement.

> "The Chilean system has served as the inspiration for 17 countries that have decided to get rid of their underfinanced systems of [retirement] distribution."

Chile's Private Pension System Is a Good Model

Universia Knowledge@Wharton

The following viewpoint is excerpted from an article published by the Wharton Business School of the University of Pennsylvania on its Universia Knowledge@Wharton Web site, an online business resource. The viewpoint features the judgments of Olivia Mitchell—an expert on Social Security at the school—and of Latin American experts, regarding the Chilean pension system. The viewpoint describes the pluses and minuses of the system's individual pension accounts, funded by contributions that are mandatory for most workers. Overall, the viewpoint presents the perspective that Chile's system is a strong, though not perfect, model with lessons for other countries' reform efforts.

As you read, consider the following questions:

1. According to Olivia Mitchell, as cited in the viewpoint, why are many pension systems heading toward financial difficulty?

2. What are the three pillars of Chile's "multi-pillar" pension system, as described in the viewpoint?

3. According to researcher Roberto Fuentes, as cited in the viewpoint, how much had Chilean workers saved in private pension accounts by 2005?

Chile's pension system, based on obligatory individual accounts and private administration, is once again a focus of attention, now that [then] U.S. President George W. Bush has presented it as a model [in 2005] for modernizing his country's Social Security system.

As early as April 2001, when Chilean president Ricardo Lagos visited the White House, Bush revealed his admiration for the performance of Chile's system. Bush focused on the year 2042 when, forecasters say, the U.S. Social Security system will collapse. "Our Social Security system must be modernized and I hope, Mister President, to receive some suggestions about how to do that, because you have done so well in that regard," Bush told Lagos, according to the official transcription of their meeting.

More Strengths than Weaknesses

All this scrutiny has exposed the weaknesses of the Chilean pension reforms, introduced 24 years ago when General Augusto Pinochet led the country. In Chile itself, the debate has focused on the people who remain outside the system—a problem that the Chilean government says it will fix by broadening Social Security coverage. Overall, the consensus is that the system of so-called "Pension Fund Administrators" has more strengths than weaknesses. That explains why, from

Central and South America to Eastern Europe, the Chilean system has served as the inspiration for 17 countries that have decided to get rid of their underfinanced systems of distribution.

What is the main attraction of the Chilean pension system? Olivia Mitchell executive director of Wharton [Business School's] Pension Research Council, suggests "four powerful reasons" for its popularity. First, the Chilean system was created at the beginning of the 1980s as the successor to the old state-run system, which went bankrupt. "Like Chile, many countries, including the United States, are facing the insolvency of their Social Security system. That's because their populations are aging, and their systems must pay a high level of benefits compared with a low level of revenues." Chile's experience is relevant for every country that is trying to make its system solvent again.

A second factor, says Mitchell, is that the Chilean reform includes the concept of individual capital accounts. "This feature appeals to many people who believe that governments are often unable to maintain sufficient assets to finance a retirement system." Individual accounts, argues Mitchell, can be better protected against political risks. Mitchell explains another relevant feature of Chile's approach: Its system incorporates a "security network" in the form of minimum pensions and old-age benefits guaranteed by the government. Mitchell agrees with those experts who applaud the multifaceted nature of the Chilean system and the way risks are shared in it. "Ultimately, the Chilean model has existed for more than 20 years, and its survival tends to inspire confidence," Mitchell says.

Multi-Pillar Pension Systems

This feature has been recognized by such institutions as the World Bank, which is promoting the development of pension systems that have more than just one foundation or "pillar."

Multi-pillar systems must distribute the responsibility of optimizing saving, redistribution and insurance for retirees among several bases of support. According to a study by the AFP [*Administradoras de Fondos de Pensiones*] Association (which comprises Chile's seven private-sector pension administrators), the first foundation of the Chilean model is the country's government. In its subsidiary role, the government finances a portion of the minimum pensions and all of the public-assistance pensions provided for the aged poor. The second foundation consists of the private-sector pension administrators who administer the obligatory Social Security savings. They help to relieve the burden on the government. The third pillar is Chile's workforce, which voluntarily saves, either to increase its pensions or in order to take early retirement. The mechanism for doing this is called 'voluntary provisional savings.'

Augusto Iglesias, a consultant at PrimAmerica, which does forecasting for foreign governments, shares Mitchell's view of the Chilean system. Individual accounts, says Iglesias, "permit the establishment of a direct link between those contributions that people make to the system and the benefits they derive from it. This creates incentives for people to assume responsibility for their own pensions" and can lead to a range of positive results for savings, the development of capital markets, and higher worker productivity. These factors, in turn, stimulate economic growth.

Its impact on economic growth is a key "virtue" of the Chilean model. According to Roberto Fuentes, research director at the association of private-sector administrators, the system acts like "a virtuous circle that generates wealth." All participants benefit. "The accumulation of savings in individual accounts generates fresh long-term resources for the economy. It lowers the cost of capital, generates investments, and leads to new jobs with higher salaries."

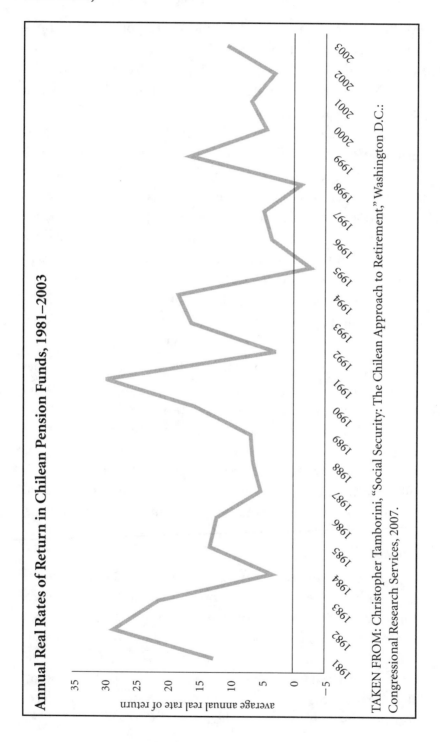

Annual Real Rates of Return in Chilean Pension Funds, 1981–2003

TAKEN FROM: Christopher Tamborini, "Social Security: The Chilean Approach to Retirement," Washington D.C.: Congressional Research Services, 2007.

Fuentes estimates that total Social Security savings of Chilean workers has reached about $60 billion, the equivalent of 60% of the country's entire GDP [gross domestic product]. Over the last 24 years, the overall return on investment for funds has been 10.3% higher than the average annual inflation rate. "As a result, 60% of old-age pensions are taken ahead of schedule. Men take early retirement nine years in advance and women take it seven years in advance."

Some Workers Left Defenseless

Critics argue that the Chilean system leaves defenseless those independent workers who do not achieve the 20 years of payments required to gain access to a minimum pension, should their funds run out. This is not a small problem. According to research by Isabel Márquez, research director at the Institute of Pension Fund Normalization [Chile's state-run pension system], in a study of 540 people registered in the system, 60.6% will not accumulate sufficient capital to get the minimum self-financed pension. Of those, 86% will also be unable to achieve the 240 contributions required to obtain a government guarantee. The country's income levels make this situation worse. According to Márquez, 50.8% of all workers who belong to the system have incomes below 200,000 Chilean pesos a month (about $340.)

What can be done? Iglesias says there is no effective way to impose Social Security contributions on independent workers. As a result, they can easily evade any possible obligation that they contribute. "If we want to increase coverage rates in this group, we have to create tax incentives for voluntary saving for Social Security, mainly by lowering taxes and by giving subsidies." Nevertheless, Iglesias warns that even this approach has limited potential. Saving for Social Security will always have a disadvantage compared with other, more liquid forms of savings, which can be used, if necessary, to finance other goals.

The problem should be tackled from another angle, says Iglesias. For many workers, housing is the main asset they can dispose of when they retire. "Nevertheless, there are no financial instruments in today's market that enable them to make this form of savings 'liquid' without losing their right to use the actual real estate—at least, not until their death." In his view, "reverse mortgages" could help solve this problem.

A System in Transition

Fuentes argues that Chile's pension system is in transition. "Most people who are now eligible for a pension contributed to the old system for a significant period of time. They are not merely getting pensions from the new system." According to studies conducted by trade unions, the new system will deliver pensions of between 70% and 105% of an average worker's income. "From the point of view of social security, that is a very good rate of return," Fuentes says.

According to Iglesias, some participants in the new system have low pensions because they did not make any contributions for long periods of time. "Nevertheless, this is not because of the Social Security system itself. It stems from that person's working career. In fact, every [Social Security] system that pays out pensions in return for worker contributions links a worker's total benefits to the contributions that he or she makes over his or her active years."

Early on, Chilean industry saw the need to increase its return on investment, improve the diversification of its portfolio and yield higher returns. This happened, largely as a result of investing in overseas markets, which now attract 30% of all Chilean funds.

People also complain about the cost of the system. Often, they are concerned about the portion of their taxable salary that is used to finance it. These funds go to managing the pension plan's savings and financing the disability and survival benefits that all Chilean firms must provide for their employees. The system also sets fixed commissions as well as variable fees that the seven public administrators use to gain a competitive edge. Mitchell admits that the system has suffered from high administrative costs and a lack of alternative investments. However, she notes, "both defects have been dramatically improved." The average commission paid by participants in Chile is 2.31% of taxable income, quite a good rate compared with the Latin American norm. According to a recent report by the World Bank, the cost of administering social security in Chile is the lowest in the region. The average participant in Chile pays 27% less than the Latin American average, and 48% less than in Mexico, where costs are highest.

Cost of Going Private

Is the United States prepared to bear the significant initial costs involved in transforming a public system into a private one, given the large U.S. budget deficit? Although the U.S. does not enjoy the fiscal surplus that Chile enjoyed when it changed its system, Mitchell believes that this should not become an obstacle on the road to urgently needed reform.

Over the years, politicians in the U.S. and many other countries have promised Social Security benefits to workers, but they have never explained how these benefits will be paid for. "A large number of honest officials need precise data, and a debate about this is taking place in the Congress," says Mitchell. "We have to reach some sort of agreement about what portion of the GDP can—and must—be used for dealing with the problem that retirees are living longer. This is especially so when governments have a lot of other national objectives, including education, health, regulation and defense. Every country will find its own balance. Chile shows us one way to do it."

Putting things in perspective, Mitchell recalls that the insolvent liabilities of the U.S. Social Security system are as large as the country's GDP (in current value). Add to that commitments for medical care for retirees, and the total cost rises to seven times the GDP. As a result, insists Mitchell, the U.S. must reform its system. A member of the presidential commission for strengthening Social Security, Mitchell believes that the investment needed for establishing the new system is affordable—less than 1% of GDP, assuming the highest level of spending. "In the final analysis, reform cannot be avoided, and the faster we act, the less painful it will be."

"Among the [Chilean] system's greatest problems are high administrative costs."

Chile's Pension System Has Numerous Problems

Christopher Tamborini

Christopher Tamborini is a Social Security analyst with the Congressional Research Service. He discusses Chile's individual pension accounts in the following viewpoint. Tamborini's research shows the positive aspects of the Chilean system, such as better than expected return on investment in private accounts, but also problems such as irregular contribution to accounts, especially by low-income or informally employed workers. Such problems, he argues, will necessitate increasing numbers of government-paid "top ups"—taxpayer financed supplements to retirement incomes—in future years. He concludes that privatization in the Chilean system has thus failed to achieve a primary goal: putting the pension system on a sustainable footing.

As you read, consider the following questions:

1. For the average Chilean worker paying into an account between 1982 and 2002, how much of the contributions to his or her pension account has been consumed by administrative fees, in Tamborini's view?

Christopher Tamborini, *Social Security: The Chilean Approach to Retirement.* Washington, DC: Congressional Research Service, 2007.

2. Out of a forty-year work life, how many years does the average Chilean contribute to his or her pension account, according to the author?

3. What are some factors Tamborini describes that explain the low participation rate in Chile's privatized pension program?

In May 1981, Chile replaced its state-run, PAYGO [pay-as-you-go] system with a private, fully funded individual retirement accounts system. The switch had a number of goals, including to restore the long-term financial balance of the system; to provide efficiency gains in the system; to reduce inequities of the old system and cover more workers; to give workers "ownership" over their retirement resources; to increase national savings; and to stimulate the national economy.

Mandatory individual retirement accounts comprise the centerpiece of the new Chilean retirement system. Individual accounts are supplemented by a minimum guaranteed pension program, a social assistance pension program, and voluntary private savings accounts system.

Participation

Workers who entered the Chilean labor force after January 1, 1983 were no longer covered by the old system. Instead, they were required to pay a proportion of their earnings into a private pension fund; that is, the individual retirement accounts system. Participation of self-employed workers in the individual retirement accounts system was made voluntary. The police and members of the armed forces remain in their own separate system to date. Those already in the workforce when the reforms were implemented were permitted to join the new system or remain in the old one, and persons already receiving a pension continued under the old law.

Workers who switched to the new system received government-financed "recognition bonds" (*bonos de reconocimiento*) to compensate them for accrued benefits under the previous system. The recognition bond is paid out of general revenues into a worker's individual account at retirement. Its value takes into account, among other things, the life expectancy of workers and the number of years they contributed to the old system.

Workers must contribute 10% of their monthly earnings to an individual retirement account, plus an additional amount (variable percentage) for administrative fees and survivors and disability insurance. There is a monthly maximum earnings limit on contributions of 60 UFs (*unidad de fomento*)—US$2,043 as of January 2007. Contributions and interest are tax-deferred until retirement. Employers are responsible for sending the monthly contribution to workers' pension fund management companies (*Administradoras de Fondos de Pensiones*, AFPs). Employers are not required to contribute but may do so. There is an additional contribution for fees and survivors and disability insurance. . . .

In Chile, mandatory individual retirement accounts are administered by private pension fund management companies known as *Administradoras de Fondos de Pensiones* (AFPs). The design emphasizes competition between AFPs in an attempt to lower administrative costs, promote higher returns on investments, and encourage better customer service.

Workers may select one AFP to manage their mandatory retirement accounts, which are invested in a mix of stocks, bonds, and other financial instruments. Workers may switch from one AFP to another at any time. When the system began, there were 12 AFPs operating. The number of AFPs peaked to 21 in 1994, and since then, a number have merged and some have been liquidated. As of January 2007, six pension fund management companies were in operation. . . .

System Financing

A primary rationale for moving to a fully funded system in Chile was that it would help the retirement system achieve solvency. The transition to an individual retirement accounts system from a PAYGO system, however, has proved fiscally expensive for Chile in the short term. During the first five years of the reforms in Chile, total transition costs—expenditures for current pensioners and for those who remained in the old system, plus the costs of redeeming recognition bonds—ranged from 4.2% to 4.7% of GDP [gross domestic product] per year, according to the Congressional Budget Office (CBO). Transition costs peaked in the late 1980s, and during the 1990s averaged roughly 4.1% of GDP annually. The entire transition period in Chile is not expected to end until about 2050—the year that benefits to those who stayed in the old system are projected to cease completely.

Another area of concern relates to new fiscal burdens on the government resulting from the growth of minimum pension guarantees (not including the proposed expansion of the program). As Chile's individual retirement accounts system matures, forecasts project that an increasing number of future retirees will qualify for a minimum pension guarantee as many current workers are not accumulating enough in their mandatory individual accounts to fund at least a minimum pension at retirement. The share of individual account holders requiring a "top up" benefit to provide a minimum pension level is projected to increase to more than 30 percent as the system matures, costing the government up to 1% of GDP.

It is worthwhile to point out several strategies that helped the Chilean government finance the transition costs, especially during the early and most expensive years of implementation. These included increasing taxes on consumption, selling a large array of state-owned enterprises, borrowing from the public, and tightening spending. These methods helped Chile build a substantial budget surplus prior to the reform (5.5% of GDP in 1980). According to the CBO, "in general, the Chilean privatization has been quite successful in managing the transition from a pay-as-you-go to a fully funded privatized retirement system."

Efficiency and Costs to Participants

Chile's switch to individual retirement accounts was also intended to improve the efficiencies of the old system. However, among the current system's greatest problems are high administrative costs. The extent of administrative costs has become a focal point of controversy in Chile because management fees reduce workers' net investment over their working lives and hence their final pension from the individual accounts. If administrative costs are reduced, more of workers' contributions can be invested (in their IAs [individual accounts]) and therefore raise the accumulated capital in their individual accounts.

Studies have shown that the cumulative impact of administrative charges on a workers' final capital accumulation and pension in Chile may be substantial. Over time it has been estimated that administrative fees have consumed a quarter (25%) of the accumulations of an average Chilean worker who began contributing in 1982 and retired in 2002. Administrative charges also reduce workers' rate of return. Estimates from the Superintendent of Pension Fund Management Companies (SAFP) have indicated that when commission fees are considered, average annual returns on Chilean pension funds between July 1981 and August 2001 decline from 10.83% to 7.33% for low earners and 7.59% for high earners. The disparity between high and low earners stems from a flat-fee on monthly contributions that exists in most AFPs. Unlike proportional fees, fixed charges tend to be regressive.

There are a number of reasons for high administrative costs in the Chilean system. Given pension fund managers' incentive to entice plan members to their AFP, the system, especially in the 1990s, experienced high marketing costs and a dramatic growth in sales personnel. Increased advertising and sales representatives also led individual participants to change AFPs excessively, thereby increasing total operating costs. A lack of competition and market transparency may also contribute to high administrative costs. From the inception of the

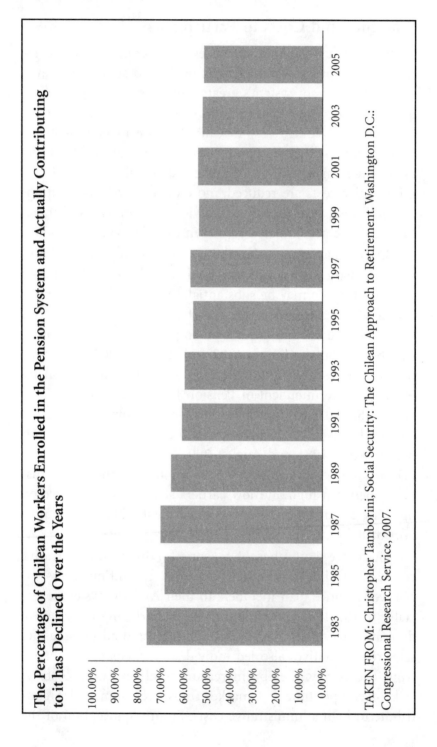

The Percentage of Chilean Workers Enrolled in the Pension System and Actually Contributing to it has Declined Over the Years

TAKEN FROM: Christopher Tamborini, Social Security: The Chilean Approach to Retirement. Washington D.C.: Congressional Research Service, 2007.

program until present, there has been a concentration of assets in a few AFPs. In July 2006, two out of the six total AFPs controlled roughly 66% of all fund assets. High administrative costs and industry concentration may have resulted from government regulation in the AFP system (e.g., regulation of fee structure, legal barriers to entry such as start-up requirements or minimum reserve fund).

Furthermore, many Chilean workers do not to appear to be well-informed about the fees associated with their individual retirement accounts. A high level of knowledge about administrative charges, some argue, may boost competition in the AFP system by encouraging more plan members to shop around for the AFP with the lowest fee structure. A recent analysis conducted by two Chilean pension experts shows that only 3.7% of plan members were aware of variable commissions charged by AFPs (and hence unable to compare fees and performance), and 52% did not know what percentage of their income went toward contributions into an individual retirement account. . . .

Lower-than-Expected Participation

The individual retirement accounts system was expected to improve participation rates in Chile, in part by linking benefits more tightly to contributions. However, active participation in the new system remains lower than expected. Whereas almost the entire Chilean workforce is enrolled in the AFP system, the share of persons actively contributing to their accounts is much smaller. In 2003 approximately 62% of the Chilean labor force, or 68% of those employed, are estimated to have contributed to their individual retirement accounts. This figure is roughly similar to the level of coverage provided under Chile's old PAYGO retirement system in the mid-1970s.

Furthermore, not all of those that actively contribute to their accounts at one point in time will contribute to them regularly over their working life. One study estimates that an average Chilean worker entering the labor force at 20 years old and retiring at 60 years old will have 21 years of contributions. Another study estimates that an average plan member makes contributions for about 54% of his/her potential working life. While around one fifth of plan members make contributions nearly 100% of the time over their careers, a substantial portion of the population does not make regular contributions. Individuals may not contribute regularly for various reasons, such as interruptions in employment or job seasonality, non-employment, and low wages in relation to daily expenses over a lifetime.

These trends reflect a growing concern in Chile that the current system does not cover the entire labor force and provides inadequate benefits to an important segment of workers. According to a Chilean government's study baseline projection, nearly 40% of workers affiliated with an AFP will accumulate enough capital to fund a benefit above the minimum level, 10% will qualify for a minimum benefit "top up" [compensatory payment from the government], and nearly half will reach retirement with less than the minimum pension and fewer than 20 years of contributions.

Several factors help explain why participation in the Chilean individual retirement accounts system has not been greater. The labor market in Chile has a high share of self-employed workers, roughly 27% of the labor force, and a large informal sector. The participation rate for self-employed workers (which is voluntary) dropped from 12% to 7% between 1986 and 2003, while salaried workers rose from 63% to 76%. Chilean men contribute to their accounts almost 40% more months than women, who work fewer years, experience interrupted periods of employment due to child rearing and have lower lifetime earnings. Another factor may be the minimum pension guarantee, which may create incentives for lower income workers to contribute just long enough to qualify for the minimum pension (20 years), and soon thereafter stop making contributions.

No Universal Solution

Obtaining knowledge of other countries' experience with reforms in their social insurance programs has gained importance in recent years as policymakers contemplate how to address Social Security's long-term financial challenges. It is difficult, however, to draw general lessons from one country's experience, as there is no universal solution to reform. Social security systems operate differently in different countries; each faces its own unique set of political and socioeconomic conditions and has a different set of income support programs for the elderly. Moreover, what is viewed as successful or desirable in one country may not be in another. Nevertheless, information of reformed retirement systems around the globe can provide valuable insight to policymakers.

The performance of Chile's individual retirement accounts system is mixed. Individual retirement accounts have contributed to the Chilean economy in a number of ways, and the returns on pension fund investments have been greater than expected. The system seems to work well for workers with stable jobs who contribute regularly to their accounts over their working lives. However, the transition to an individual retirement accounts system has proved fiscally expensive for Chile. Concerns remain about low participation rates, especially among women and low-income workers, including members of the informal sector. Analysts also agree that administrative costs have been too high.

Periodical Bibliography

The following articles have been selected to supplement the diverse views presented in this chapter.

Carlos A. Ball — "Chile: Reform Success South of the Border," *Human Events*, March 15, 2005.

Andrew G. Biggs — "Social Insecurity? Personal Accounts and the Stock Market Collapse," *AEI Online*, November 24, 2008. www.aei.org.

Norma Cohen — "A Bloody Mess," *American Prospect*, January 11, 2005.

Barbara T. Dreyfuss — "The Siren of Santiago," *Mother Jones*, March/April 2005.

Andrew Herscovitch and David Stanton — "History of Social Security in Australia," *Family Matters*, September 2008.

David C. John — "What Do Almost 40 Countries Know That We Don't?" *Human Events*, March 15, 2005.

Barbara E. Kritzer — "Chile's Next Generation Pension Reform," *Social Security Bulletin*, June 2008.

Jimmy Langman — "A Big Step to the Left," *Newsweek*, January 15, 2007.

Pensions & Investments — "An Idea Down Under," 2006.

James Schulz — "Old Age Security: Australia Tries a Different Way," *AARP Public Policy Institute*, December 2005. www.aarp.org/research/ppi/.

Jyoti Thottam — "Lessons from Overseas," *Time*, February 14, 2005.

Joseph White — "Compared to Other Countries: How Exceptional Are the Health and Income Security Arrangements of the United States?" *Generations*, Spring 2005.

For Further Discussion

Chapter 1

1. The Board of Trustees of the OASDI have projected that by the mid-2010s Social Security will begin to give out more in benefits than it receives in revenue and that in 2037 the funds in the Social Security Trust Fund will be exhausted. The National Committee to Preserve Social Security and Medicare holds that the Social Security system is in good financial shape. Which viewpoint do you think presents the more credible picture of Social Security's finances? Why?

2. Gayle L. Reznik, Dave Shoffner, and David A. Weaver point out that the problems faced by Social Security are due in large part to an aging population. Smaller families and people living longer means that there will be a shortfall in the number of younger workers, and they will be paying benefits to a growing number of retirees; how does Teresa Ghilarducci respond to this argument? Who do you think makes the better case, and why?

3. William Greider suggests that people such as Peter Peterson who claim that Social Security is in crisis are doing so because they can gain financially from changes in the system. How might businessmen benefit by creating fears of a crisis in Social Security? Why might advocacy groups like the National Committee to Preserve Social Security and Medicare want to convince the public that social security is on a sound financial footing?

Chapter 2

1. Peter A. Diamond and Peter R. Orszag believe that relatively small increases in taxes and reductions in benefits

can solve the problem of a projected shortfall in the Social Security system. What does Edgar K. Browning think is the proper solution to Social Security's problems? Does Browning base his argument purely upon economic grounds or do other considerations play a part in his position on Social Security? Explain your answer, citing from the viewpoint.

2. David C. John and Rea S. Hederman Jr. do not believe that raising the "wage cap" on Social Security payroll taxes will be an effective remedy for the system's projected shortfalls. Does John Miller believe that lifting the wage cap will completely solve Social Security's financial problems? What reasons does he give for raising the wage cap? Are they cogent reasons in your opinion? Explain your answer.

Chapter 3

1. Jennifer L. Erkulwater shows in her viewpoint that the number of disabled people receiving Social Security has grown faster than other categories of recipients. The GAO's report argues that proposed reforms in Social Security will reduce benefits to the disabled. According to Erkulwater's article, what sorts of programs might help at least some categories of disabled beneficiaries cope with proposed Social Security cuts? What positive results might be seen if direct monetary benefits to disabled people are reduced in favor of other types of support? Cite from the viewpoint in crafting your answer.

2. William E. Spriggs makes the case that African Americans receive a disproportionate amount of Social Security benefits and therefore switching to a system of privatized individual accounts will hurt the black community. How does Michael Tanner answer Spriggs's case? According to Tanner, what major benefit would a privatized system provide to African Americans that they do not receive under

Social Security? How would that benefit increase equality in American society? In your answer cite from the viewpoints.

3. Leanne Abdnor argues that privatization of Social Security would help women—particularly women who never married or who divorced after just a few years of marriage. According to Ross Prizzia, what feature of Social Security generally helps women? How might the different sorts of evidence looked at by the two authors lead to such different conclusions?

Chapter 4

1. After looking at the United Kingdom's experience with pension privatization, Alicia H. Munnell and Steven A. Sass find that the program has been a failure. In contrast James Banks and his coauthors think that while the privatized system has had troubles, it is on the whole successful. What changes does the Banks et al. viewpoint recommend to help increase the reliability of the privatized system? Do you think that Munnell and Sass would agree that such changes could rescue the British system of individual retirement accounts? Why or why not?

2. When it was first implemented, the privatization of the Chilean pension system was hailed by economists, and many still think the Chilean approach is a good model for other countries. What would author Christopher Tamborini think about the United States following Chile's example? What sorts of problems, according to Tamborini, might the United States expect if it went the privatization route?

Organizations to Contact

The editors have compiled the following list of organizations concerned with the issues debated in this book. The descriptions are derived from materials provided by the organizations. All have publications or information available for interested readers. The list was compiled on the date of publication of the present volume; the information provided here may change. Be aware that many organizations take several weeks or longer to respond to inquiries, so allow as much time as possible.

AARP Public Policy Institute

601 E Street NW, Washington, DC 20049

(202) 434-3840

e-mail: ppi@aarp.org

Web site: www.aarp.org/research/ppi

AARP is a membership organization that advocates on behalf of retired people. It has more than 40 million members in the fifty states, the District of Columbia, Puerto Rico, and the U.S. Virgin Islands. As the premier lobbying group for older Americans, the organization has a great stake in the Social Security debate; it opposes privatization if money is taken away from the current system. AARP's research arm, the Public Policy Institute (PPI), publishes research on Social Security as well as surveys of Americans' attitudes toward the system and its reform. PPI's Social Security research, grouped together under the heading "PPI Reports on Social Security," can be found on its Web site.

Brookings Institution

1775 Massachusetts Ave. NW, Washington, DC 20036

(202) 797-6000

online contact form: www.brookings.edu/about/ContactUs
.aspx
Web site: www.brookings.edu

The Brookings Institution is one of America's oldest think tanks. Originally associated with the Robert Brookings Graduate School of Economics and Government, it is now an independent research and publishing organization. It issues the *Brookings Bulletin* four times a year as well as the series Brookings Papers on Economic Activity. Examples of its work on Social Security include "Bridging the Social Security Divide: Lessons from Abroad" and "Why the 2005 Social Security Initiative Failed, and What It Means for the Future." More papers on Social Security can be found at the institution's Web site.

Cato Institute

1000 Massachusetts Ave. NW, Washington, DC 20001-5403
(202) 842-0200 • fax: (202) 842-3490
online contact form: www.catocampus.org/contact
Web site: www.cato.org

A libertarian think tank, the Cato Institute promotes the benefits of a free market and limited government. The institute takes a dim view of any kind of government interference with the economy. This includes government-run, pay-as-you-go (PAYGO) pension programs. Cato has been one of the leading proponents of Social Security privatization, what the organization calls "Social Security Choice." Its Web site includes articles such as "Privatizing Social Security: The $10 Trillion Opportunity" and "Social Security's Problems Haven't Gone Away."

Center for Budget and Policy Priorities

820 First Street NE, Suite 510, Washington, DC 20002
(202) 408-1080 • fax: (202) 408-1056
e-mail: center@cbpp.org
Web site: www.cbpp.org

This think tank sees itself as an advocate for poor and working people in the federal government's debates over spending. The center examines the effects of Social Security on poverty, including poverty among children, and on particular demographic groups. The organization's Web site hosts a variety of Social Security–related materials, including a useful introduction to the program and the debates surrounding it titled "Policy Basics: Top Ten Facts on Social Security."

Economic Policy Institute

1333 H Street NW, Suite 300, East Tower
Washington, DC   20005-4707
(202) 775-8810 • fax: (202) 775-0819
e-mail: research@epi.org
Web site: www.epi.org

The Economic Policy Institute states that its mission is "to inform people and empower them to seek solutions that will ensure broadly shared prosperity and opportunity." It is particularly concerned with improving economic conditions for working Americans. Papers and publications such as "Social Security: Here Today, Still Here Tomorrow" and "Issue Guide on Social Security" take the position that a government-run Social Security system is necessary for economic security.

The Heritage Foundation

214 Massachusetts Ave. NE, Washington, DC   20002-4999
(202) 546-4400 • fax: (202) 546-8328
e-mail: info@heritage.org
Web site: www.heritage.org

The Heritage Foundation is a conservative think tank that promotes, in the words of its mission statement, "economic opportunity, prosperity, and a flourishing civil society." The organization stresses free-market solutions to societal problems; it therefore supports the privatization of Social Security. Its Web site features publications such as "Social Security's Unexpected Deficits Show Urgent Need for Reform" and "CBO's Warning on Raising Taxes to Pay for Medicare, Medicaid, and Social Security." The foundation's essays are often analyses of official reports by the Congressional Budget Office (CBO) or the Social Security Administration, which look at the data from a free-market, conservative perspective.

Institute for Women's Policy Research

1707 L Street NW, Suite 750, Washington, DC   20036
(202) 785-5100 • fax: (202) 833-4362
e-mail: iwpr@iwpr.org
Web site: www.iwpr.org

The Institute for Women's Policy Research focuses on issues of poverty and welfare, employment and earnings, work and family issues, and health and safety from women's perspective. It also seeks to boost women's civic and political participation. Two examples of its Social Security–related publications are: "Why Privatizing Social Security Would Hurt Women" and "Social Security: The Largest Source of Income for Both Women and Men in Retirement." The organization has an e-mail alert service that will notify interested individuals when it publishes new reports.

Joint Center for Political and Economic Studies

1090 Vermont Ave. NW, Suite 1100
Washington, DC   20005-4928
(202) 789-3500 • fax: (202) 789-6385
e-mail: general@jointcenter.org
Web site: www.jointcenter.org

The Joint Center for Political and Economic Studies is a research and public policy institute whose work focuses on issues of concern to African Americans and other people of color. The center is particularly strong in presenting the results of surveys showing how Social Security affects the African American community. Some examples are: "Retirement Prospects and Perils: Public Opinion on Social Security and Wealth, by Race 1997–2005" and "Social Security and Wealth: Fact Sheet About African Americans by Income Group." These and many other Social Security–related publications are available on the center's Web site.

The Urban Institute Retirement Policy Program

2100 M Street NW, Washington, DC   20037
(202) 833-7200

online contact form: www.urban.org/about/contact.cfm
Web site: www.retirementpolicy.org

The Urban Institute's Retirement Policy Program "provides objective, nonpartisan guidance to policy-makers through its analyses of how current government policies, private sector practices, and demographic trends influence older Americans' security and decision making." Generally considered on the center-left of the political spectrum, the institute has published "Social Security: Out of Step with the Modern Family" and "Social Security in an Age of Uncertainty," as well as transcripts of its researchers' testimony about Social Security before Congressional committees.

U.S. Government Accountability Office (GAO)

441 G Street NW, Washington, DC 20548
(202) 512-3000
e-mail: contact@gao.gov
Web site: http://gao.gov

According to its Web site, the "GAO investigates how the federal government spends taxpayer dollars." Previously named the Government Accounting Office, the GAO is also tasked with projecting future spending requirements and determining how changes in government programs will affect specific groups in American society. In fulfilling these two tasks the office has published a wealth of reports on Social Security, particularly on the program's future financial state and on how proposed reforms would affect women and minority groups. The majority of reports completed after 1998 are online at the GAO's Web site.

U.S. Social Security Administration, Office of Research, Evaluation, and Statistics

500 E Street SW, 8th Floor, Washington, DC 20254
(202) 358-6276 • fax: (202) 358-6192
e-mail: op.publications@ssa.gov
Web site: www.ssa.gov

The Social Security Administration's Office of Research, Evaluation, and Statistics is the premier source for data and statistics on how much money Social Security receives from payroll taxes and how much it pays out in benefits. A wealth of historical data allows students or researchers to analyze how the program has changed over the years. Those using the office's resources may want to familiarize themselves with Social Security's operations and history before seeking information directly from this organization. Detailed official statistics can be accessed directly at www.ssa.gov/policy/research.html.

Bibliography of Books

Robert Asen   *Invoking the Invisible Hand: Social Security and the Privatization Debates.* East Lansing: Michigan State University Press, 2009.

Jeffrey K. Bain   *Social Security Solvency.* New York: Nova Science, 2009.

Daniel Béland   *Social Security: History and Politics from the New Deal to the Privatization Debate.* Lawrence: University Press of Kansas, 2005.

Christoph Borgmann   *Social Security, Demographics, and Risk.* New York: Springer, 2005.

J. Larry Brown, Robert Kuttner, and Thomas M. Shapiro   *Building a Real "Ownership Society."* New York: Century Foundation, 2005.

Edgar K. Browning   *Stealing from Each Other: How the Welfare State Robs Americans of Money and Spirit.* Westport, CT: Praeger, 2008.

Andrew W. Dobelstein   *Understanding the Social Security Act: The Foundation of Social Welfare for America in the Twenty-first Century.* New York: Oxford University Press, 2009.

Robert Stowe England   *The Fiscal Challenge of an Aging Industrial World.* Washington, DC: Center for Strategic and International Studies, 2002.

Don Fullerton and Brent D. Mast	*Income Redistribution from Social Security.* Washington, DC: AEI Press, 2005.
Melissa A. Hardy, and Lawrence E. Hazelrigg	*Pension Puzzles: Social Security and the Great Debate.* New York: Russell Sage Foundation, 2007.
Michael J. Hill	*Social Policy in the Modern World: A Comparative Text.* Malden, MA: Blackwell, 2006.
Robert B. Hudson	*The New Politics of Old Age Policy.* Baltimore: Johns Hopkins University Press, 2005.
Estelle James, Alejandra Cox Edwards, and Rebeca Wong	*The Gender Impact of Social Security Reform.* Chicago: University of Chicago Press, 2008.
Alain Jousten and the International Monetary Fund Fiscal Affairs Dept.	*Public Pension Reform: A Primer.* Washington, DC: International Monetary Fund, 2007.
Stephen J. Kay and Tapen Sinha	*Lessons from Pension Reform in the Americas.* New York: Oxford University Press, 2008.
Patrik Marier	*Pension Politics: Consensus and Social Conflict in Ageing Societies.* New York: Routledge, 2008.
Ailsa McKay	*The Future of Social Security Policy: Women, Work and a Citizens' Basic Income.* New York: Routledge, 2005.

Mike O'Brien   *Poverty, Policy and the State: Social Security Reform in New Zealand.* Bristol, UK: Policy, 2008.

Mitchell A. Orenstein   *Pensions, Social Security, and the Privatization of Risk.* New York: Columbia University Press, 2009.

Mary Poole   *The Segregated Origins of Social Security: African Americans and the Welfare State.* Chapel Hill: University of North Carolina Press, 2006.

Rachel Pruchno and Michael A. Smyer   *Challenges of an Aging Society: Ethical Dilemmas, Political Issues.* Baltimore: Johns Hopkins University Press, 2007.

Leonard Jay Santow and Mark E. Santow   *Social Security and the Middle Class Squeeze: Fact and Fiction About America's Entitlement Programs.* Westport, CT: Praeger, 2005.

Max J. Skidmore   *Securing America's Future: A Bold Plan to Preserve and Expand Social Security.* Lanham, MD: Rowman & Littlefield, 2008.

Carol Weisbrod   *Grounding Security: Family, Insurance and the State.* Burlington, VT: Ashgate, 2006.

Index

A

Abdnor, Leanne, 158–164

Accumulated assets, 29, 30, 33, 88, 91–92

Administradoras de Fondos de Pensiones (AFP), 185, 193, 195–197, 198

Advisory Council on Social Security, 37

African Americans
  anti-poverty program for, 134–135, 139
  benefits to, 141, 143–144, 146–148
  as disabled persons, 143
  income gap with, 146–147
  inheritable wealth and, 147–148
  life-expectancy of, 137–138, 144, 146
  privatization and, 136, 145–146
  as seniors, 135–137
  Social Security and, 116, 118, 138–139, 142, 144–145
  wealth-building by, 133–134

Aging populations
  benefits for, 37, 38, 62, 152
  demographic changes to, 35–36, 62–63
  implications of, 58–60
  in industrial countries, 19
  PAYGO and, 59
  pension reforms for, 60–61
  postponing retirement, 64
  support for, 62–64
  women and, 153

work capacity of, 42–44
  See also Elderly people

Agricultural workers, 142–143

American Association of Retired Persons (AARP), 96, 109

American Association of University Women (AAUW), 152

American social insurance, 66–67, 74

Annual surplus, 29, 31–33

Anti-poverty program, 134–135, 139

Australia, pension plans, 58, 167–168

B

Baby-boom generation
  cost-saving measures and, 145
  fertility rates of, 36
  generation after, 44
  payroll taxes and, 16
  retirement of, 19, 23, 50, 74, 78, 126, 144–145

Baker, Dean, 54, 148

Bakja, Jan, 137

Bankruptcy fears
  exaggeration of, 20, 32–33
  financial strength and, 27–33
  future outlook, 22–24
  over government borrowing, 32
  solvency options, 37–39

Banks, James, 175–181

Basic State Pension (U.K.), 170–173, 176, 178

Baxter, Marianne, 160–161